SHAPING
THE HEART

Published by
The Bible Reading Fellowship
15 The Chambers, Vineyard
Abingdon OX14 3FE
United Kingdom
Tel: +44 (0)1865 319700
Email: enquiries@brf.org.uk
Website: www.brf.org.uk
BRF is a Registered Charity

ISBN 978 1 84101 726 6
First published 2011
10 9 8 7 6 5 4 3 2 1 0
All rights reserved

Acknowledgments
Unless otherwise stated, scripture quotations are taken from the Holy Bible, New International
Version, © 1973, 1978, 1984 by International Bible Society, and are used by permission
of Hodder and Stoughton Limited. All rights reserved. 'NIV' is a registered trade mark of
International Bible Society. UK trademark number 1448790.

Scripture taken from THE MESSAGE. Copyright © Eugene H. Peterson, 1993, 1994, 1995. Used
by permission of Navpress Publishing Group.

Scripture taken from *The New Testament in Modern English*. Copyright © by J.B. Phillips, 1960.
Used by permission of HarperCollins Publishers.

Scripture taken from The Amplified Bible, New Testament copyright © 1958, 1987 The
Lockman Foundation. Used by permission.

Extracts from the Authorized Version of the Bible (The King James Bible), the rights in which
are vested in the Crown, are reproduced by permission of the Crown's Patentee, Cambridge
University Press.

New King James Version copyright © 1985 Thomas Nelson Inc.

Extract from The Living Bible copyright © Tyndale House Publishers 1971.

Scriptures quoted from the Good News Bible published by The Bible Societies/HarperCollins
Publishers Ltd, UK © American Bible Society 1966, 1971, 1976, 1992, used with permission.

Scripture quotations from the Complete Jewish Bible, copyright 1998 by David H. Stern.
Published by Jewish New Testament Publications, Inc. www.messianicjewish.net/jntp.
Distributed by Messianic Jewish Resources Int'l. www.messianicjewish.net. All rights reserved.
Used by permission.

The paper used in the production of this publication was supplied by mills that source their
raw materials from sustainably managed forests. Soy-based inks were used in its printing and
the laminate film is biodegradable.

A catalogue record for this book is available from the British Library

Printed in Singapore by Craft Print International Ltd

SHAPING THE HEART

Reflections on spiritual formation and fruitfulness

PAMELA EVANS

ACKNOWLEDGMENTS

It would be impossible to list all who have contributed in diverse ways during the very long gestation of this book. However, I'd like to record my thanks to Jan Acton, Lin Button, Paul Bradbury, Helen East, Stephen Evans and Chris Key. Their detailed comments on drafts during the last few months of writing sharpened my thinking and, I trust, helped me to communicate more effectively. Some material was previewed in teaching within my own church family. I hope they already know how much I appreciate their feedback and encouragement.

To say that writing a book of this nature is challenging would be an understatement. I am particularly grateful to Lin Button, Margaret Milborrow and Andrea Williams who have faithfully accompanied me on the journey and encouraged me in my commitment to 'walk the talk'.

Fourteen years ago, BRF Commissioning Editor Naomi Starkey's enthusiasm for working with a new author was a breath of fresh air after gloomy responses from elsewhere. Since then, I've valued her gracious and good-humoured persistence in bringing to my attention features of good writing with which I might otherwise never have become acquainted! The BRF team has been a pleasure to work with, and I continue to thank God for them.

PREFACE

This book is just a tool. To be of any benefit, it must be *used*. Rushing through on an intellect-only, fact-finding mission will defeat its purpose. It's for brothers and sisters in Christ who are seeking more fruitful discipleship, not just better informed discipleship. Fruitful discipleship comes from yielding to the Spirit of truth and welcoming God's grace *over time*, within a growing relationship with our heavenly Father.

'Be transformed…' wrote Paul to the Christians in Rome (Romans 12:2), and he says the same to us today. However, this isn't a self-help book. If there is such a thing, it's a God-help-me book; after all, spiritual transformation is God's work. It's designed to increase awareness of the nourishment our heavenly Father provides for the Christ-life in us and of the part he calls us to play, which is to open our hearts to him, to welcome his provision, and to cooperate, not hinder, as he makes us more like Jesus.

I'm going to assume that you've already met Christ in the scriptures and welcomed him as both Saviour and Lord. I'm also assuming that Jesus is the one on whom, in your finer moments at least, you wish to be modelled.

The chapter headings give an overall idea of the ground to be covered. There isn't one chapter focusing on reading the Bible because the shaping effect of the scriptures will be acknowledged in every chapter. Neither is there one devoted to the value of Christian fellowship because, throughout, we'll be noting the way we both shape and are shaped by those around us. The book could be used in a home group or discipleship group with this in mind.

Some of the 'reflections' mentioned in the subtitle are mine, but the rest will, I hope, be yours. At the end of each chapter, three Bible reflections are offered as springboards into further dialogue with God; for these, you'll need a Bible. If you're taking the book on retreat, you could use all three reflections during the course of a day, maybe keeping a record of what God says to you in a journal or notebook. If reading is being fitted in between other demands, then use as many as you are able; at least one per chapter will be suitable for mulling over while travelling to work, having tea breaks or washing up. If you're not sharing the book with a group, you might find it helpful to explore a reflection or two in the company of a spiritual director or mentor.

So now you know where we're heading, I invite you to take a deep breath... and read on.

CONTENTS

INTRODUCTION

In an age in which 'style matters' and appearances so often hold sway over substance, why should I spend time attending to my inner life? The short answer is that the scriptures see it as important: while 'man looks at the outward appearance… the Lord looks at the heart' (1 Samuel 16:7). Medical campaigners champion the cause of the physical heart, for the sake of quality of life as well as longevity. The Great Physician would also have us attend to our inner being, to that other 'heart', which includes the mind and the will. He wants us to open this heart to his scrutiny and to apply his wise counsel on how to care for it. The book of Proverbs says, '*Above all else*, guard your heart, for it is the wellspring of life' (4:23, italics mine). If I'm committed to following God's declared priorities, that's the issue resolved, then!

Far from being the preserve of those in ivory towers or hermit cells, matters relating to spiritual formation and transformation, and to character development, are foundational to Christian life and faith in every context and at every level— and these processes necessarily involve the heart. Throughout the book, they'll be referred to in ways designed to draw in those for whom these aspects of discipleship are unfamiliar, while also extending the grasp of those who are at home in such areas.

Our hearts are, among other things, the arenas for the battle to learn to trust, and the places in which habits (godly or otherwise) are eventually solidified into character. God created them to be worship-filled, holy places with himself in residence; gardens in which the fruit of his Spirit may grow. If you wished, you could take a moment to talk to God about the state of your (his) 'house and garden' before continuing.

In formation

Whoever we are, and wherever we grow up, the messages we receive—from our family, our community and the world around us—contribute to the shaping of our inner life. Unspoken assumptions and attitudes, and the value systems we see being lived out in the habits of others, have greater influence than instructions to do or not do, to be or not be something. Philosopher and theologian Dallas Willard has written extensively on spiritual formation and has emphasised that it is 'a process that happens to everyone. The most despicable as well as the most admirable... Terrorists as well as saints are the outcome of spiritual formation' (*Renovation of the Heart*, p. 19).

In infancy we have little control but, year on year, the part played by our own choices increases. Even if, as adults, we choose to limit our deliberate spiritual intake to mainstream Christian truth and practice (and let's not get distracted here by possible definitions of 'mainstream', 'Christian', 'truth' and 'practice'), we receive many other forms of input during our waking hours. Most of us underestimate these unbidden and often barely detectable influences and their potential for moulding us in ways that may undermine a desire to become more like Christ. For example, in the media, 'experts' hold forth on matters of life, faith and everything, and tell us what and how to be, but characters in soap operas also teach subliminally what is or is not 'cool', 'normal' or to be feared. The lapping of this insidious tide can be surprisingly influential, not only on our thinking but also on our hearts' responses to people and to the options open to us.

Paul urged first-century Christians, 'Don't let the world around you squeeze you into its own mould' (Romans 12:2, J.B. Phillips). Disciples who allow their hearts to be fed indiscriminately, to be nourished haphazardly, to be shaped by whatever happens to be surrounding them at the time, will struggle to remain faithful. Paul's advice is not an instruction to head for an enclosed community within which to escape pollution—as if that were possible! No, now as then, it's a call to be more alert to what is happening to our inner being as we work, spend time with friends and family, pursue leisure activities, travel and so on. Paul continued, 'Let God re-mould your minds from within, so that you may prove in practice that the plan of God for you is good, meets all his demands and moves towards the goal of true maturity.' 'True maturity': is that something we're praying for God to bring into being in one another?

Regrettably, it's not only what is happening 'out there' that serves to undermine rather than facilitate God's plans for bringing out the best in his children. Of obvious concern is the fact that some believers are prepared to appraise the value or success of a church in terms of its activity programme without reference to the state of its members' hearts. The bumper sticker 'Jesus is coming back—look busy!' may have started out as a joke but finds too many resonances in churches today to be truly funny.

So, you have already been spiritually formed; your friends from church and your neighbours have already been spiritually formed; and the process is continuing, even as you read. You could pause to consider this question: in practice, day by day in real life, *who or what is shaping the way I think, feel and live*? Stick with the question for a while—maybe also asking your nearest and dearest for their perspective. Probably the only answer that is both short *and* true is 'Lots of things'. Cistercian monk Thomas Merton wrote, 'Every moment and every event of every man's life on earth plants something in his soul.' He continued, 'If I were looking for God, every event and every moment would sow, in my will, grains of His life that would spring up one day in a tremendous harvest' (*New Seeds of Contemplation*, pp. 14, 16). Why not enter into dialogue with God about the question, and about whether the answers that come to mind sit comfortably with his plans for your transformation? The range of influences currently shaping you may come as a surprise.

Looking back

In Chapter 1, you'll be invited to examine the building blocks of character that were set in place, constructively or haphazardly, for good or for ill, during your early years. If you're a parent, this might prompt you to reflect on how your own children are being formed, and what they're consuming. For all of us, it's worth considering the effect we may be having on the lives of children and young adults in our communities. William Inge, Dean of St Paul's Cathedral, London, in the first part of the 20th century, is often quoted as having said,

'The proper time to influence the character of a child is about a hundred years before he is born.' How mindful are we today of the inheritance we're laying down for future generations in our family, town, nation and world?

'Train a child in the way he should go, and when he is old he will not turn from it' (Proverbs 22:6). A century ago, it was accepted that building good character in children was a worthy task, and one to which all men and women of goodwill—not just clergy and school teachers—would contribute. The aim was that every child would grow into an adult with a sense of the difference between right and wrong, an internalised 'moral compass' pointing them towards honest living and truthful dealing. The quotation from Proverbs is a generalisation, not a guarantee; some choose to ignore their moral compass. However, the importance of building good character was generally accepted and, in most of the Western world, the understanding of 'good character' and the language used to speak about it came from the scriptures.

Much has changed. In his book *The Death of Character*, James Davison Hunter reviews the transformation in attitudes and practices in the United States of America during the 20th century. World War I was followed by an era in which psychological humanism became a powerful influence within the educational establishment; religion was increasingly trivialised. Hunter charts the rise of progressivism, which steered away from developing moral character and towards promoting individual psychological well-being. Teachers were instructed to encourage children to develop their own personalities and moral frameworks and, while doing so, not to cramp any child's individual style. The traditional approach of training children to develop good habits and become good citizens was discredited. After all, the reasoning went, in progressive and enlightened times, who is to say what 'good' means? And, the argument continued, the personal growth and achievements of the individual are paramount; nurturing community is old hat.

Most of us have imbibed and been shaped by these 'progressive' and psychology-driven schemes to a greater extent than we know. Our communities have certainly been affected by them, and by other supposedly forward-looking influences. Those who remember 'how it used to be' yearn for the days when doors could safely be left unlocked and a gentleman's word was his bond. In the United Kingdom, citizenship lessons have been added to the school curriculum but these alone will be insufficient to redress the balance. Hunter sees contemporary society impaled on the horns of a dilemma:

We want character but without unyielding conviction; we want strong morality but without the emotional burden of guilt or shame; we want virtue but without particular moral justifications that invariably offend; we want good without having to name evil; we want decency without the authority to insist upon it; we want moral community without any limitations to personal freedom. In short, we want what we cannot possibly have on the terms that we want it.

JAMES DAVISON HUNTER, *THE DEATH OF CHARACTER*, P. XV

So where do we go from here? Is it possible to turn the clock back? And do we really want to? Much that happened in the past was far from good. I shall come back to this later, but I want to make it clear now that I have no wish to see a return to some of the child-rearing practices of 100 years ago, especially the old shame-based teaching methods still employed by some in my younger days. I also welcome many of the insights brought by psychology, although, as I've studied the Bible over the years, I've been struck by how many of the so-called modern psychological insights were previewed there. (See how many you can spot in the course of your own Bible reading.)

The main problem lies with responses to the psychological insights—particularly when they've been used to justify sweeping aside the biblical foundations that undergirded the lives of ordinary folk a century ago. Back then, even those whose life-choices took no account of God had, to a considerable extent, internalised and been unwittingly shaped by the scriptures and the view of truth and reality contained therein. How different for the majority of today's 20- and 30-somethings! Their parents grew up in a different climate, internalising different assumptions, and we're beginning to see the consequences in the lives of their children and grandchildren.

To return to my most recent questions: no, I don't think it's possible to turn back the clock, but within our spheres of influence it *is* possible to be agents for change. As we do so, we may carry with us that other question, 'Who or what is shaping the way I think, feel and live?' We may also reflect on how Father God is seeking to use everyday events and encounters as shaping tools, as part of his ongoing project to transform us into the men and women he created us to be and to make us more like Jesus.

Becoming more like Christ

Jesus is the very expression of God's essence. He is described as 'the image [Greek: *eikon*] of the invisible God' (Colossians 1:15); 'the radiance of God's glory and the exact representation [Greek: *charakter*] of his being' (Hebrews 1:3). During his earthly life, Jesus uniquely bore the imprint of God's nature; those who had seen him had 'seen the Father' (John 14:9). Yet, in the beginning, men and women were created in God's image (Genesis 1:27; the image was swiftly marred). As we allow the Father to bring to birth in us our born-again heredity as children of God, and as we yield to the restoring work of his Holy Spirit and welcome 'the glistening purity of Jesus' life as a model for our own' (1 John 3:3, *THE MESSAGE*), we become more as God intended and less like the marred image with which we are all more familiar. Members of the family known as the body of Christ are *all* image-bearers in the process of restoration (see, for example, 2 Corinthians 3:18).

The world over, we expect children to share characteristics with their parents and siblings, and in God's family that's meant to be normal, too. When we are born again of the Spirit (John 3:3–8), that is, 'born of God', 'God's seed' (Greek: *sperma*) remains in us (1 John 3:9). This assures us that we are his children and enables us to show the family likeness. Gradually, we become more conscious of elder brother Jesus walking alongside, and of his attitudes and *modus operandi*.

It isn't simply a matter of our copying Jesus in the way small brothers and sisters copy older siblings. It's a matter of 'becoming'—allowing our new (born-again) heredity to manifest itself; allowing Christ to be formed in us (Galatians 4:19); welcoming the Holy Spirit, the bringer of the family likeness. As we make the day-by-day choices necessary for our new life to flourish, and take full advantage of the nourishment and training God provides for the aspects of our person that need to grow, the character of Jesus will increasingly be formed in us. The other side of the coin will be our refusal to indulge or feed those aspects that do not honour God or serve his plan for us to become more fully the people he created us to be. Father God is more ready to supply wisdom and build courage for this process than we are to ask.

John urges, 'Live deeply in Christ', adding that 'all who practise righteousness are God's true children' (1 John 2:28–29, *THE MESSAGE*). In John's Gospel, Jesus is described as being 'full of grace and truth' (1:14; see also v. 17). It's all very well thinking noble thoughts about living deeply in Christ and becoming more like him, but such ideas need to be earthed in the reality of a person's life—in *my* real life. If you dare, ask yourself, 'Am I being formed according to the heredity of the One who is righteousness, grace and truth personified? Or some other...?' Then consider a related question, which is about the 'seeds' being sown in the lives of children and others with whom you are in contact: 'Are these seeds impregnated with grace and truth or something less life-affirming?' If you know you need to seek God's forgiveness, how about doing so now? Confess what needs confessing, then ask for his cleansing and empowering as you set out on the road to godly change and living differently.

Our English word 'character' has its origins in Greek words relating to engraving—stamping with a mark. It's not at all unreasonable to ask, 'Where's the hallmark? Are those who know us seeing the resemblance to the One from whom we take our name?' Jesus made it clear to his first disciples that their lives should be revealing his nature (for example, John 13:35). Even if they didn't understand what he meant at the time, some of them later put quill to papyrus to exhort other followers of Jesus to do just that. Passages from their letters will be referred to later, especially those expanding on what Paul called 'the fruit of the Spirit' (Galatians 5:22–23).

Aspects of the fruit of the Spirit are covered towards the end of each of the first five chapters of this book. This running theme builds towards the final chapter focusing on fruitfulness. It's vital to keep in mind at every stage that the aim of spiritual transformation is not the production of well-formed exhibits for God's showcase. He seeks our cooperation as he forms us into women and men who show the family likeness, so that we may fulfil our appointed role and bear fruit for his kingdom—fruit that will demonstrate the presence and rule of Christ the king; fruit that will bring God glory and fill the earth with knowledge of him and his ways; fruit that will last. More on all that in due course.

Forgiving and forgiven

An important aspect of becoming more like Christ is learning to forgive: learning to forgive, all the time, as 'normal'; learning to forgive—full stop (see, for example, Matthew 6:12, 14–15;

Luke 23:34; Ephesians 4:32; Colossians 3:13.) Forgiving someone means choosing no longer to hold resentment against them. Our forgiveness should extend to those who have harmed us by their actions or attitudes, even when they have caused us to be in need of significant spiritual renovation. It's to include those who show no sign of remorse and those who, having said 'sorry', continue in the same way as before. 'Forgiving' someone doesn't imply that their actions were or are acceptable. Neither does it oblige us to allow them to continue to hurt us, pretending that it's not a problem. If you know that forgiving someone who has harmed you is a major issue, or if you are in an abusive relationship, I'd encourage you to seek help from an accredited Christian counsellor or a church leader with a recognised pastoral ministry.

These days, we're often advised to 'forgive ourselves'. When we've brought grief and pain to others and to God, forgiving ourselves is best understood as choosing to agree with God—that is, taking him at his word, which says, 'If we confess our sins, he is faithful and just and will forgive us our sins and purify us from all unrighteousness' (1 John 1:9). The pattern has been set for us by God: genuine repentance, followed by receiving forgiveness and moving on—leaving behind the sin he has dealt with, and heeding his instruction to 'go and sin no more'. Each of us needs to learn to work with this pattern, because it's the only one God offers. Knowing ourselves to be forgiven, laying down our burden of guilt and shame, is vital for our relationships—with God, but also with others—and essential for health, well-being and fruitful discipleship.

Pride may block our release into the joy of being forgiven.

As difficult as some find it to believe, continuing to beat themselves up over failures and offences, soldiering on in what has been called a penance of perpetual regret, is no more godly than refusing to forgive others. Both are spiritually-deforming anti-grace postures; both are abhorrent to God. He sent Jesus to die for us while we were powerless, mired in our sin (Romans 5:6–8), so that we might count ourselves dead to sin (6:6–14). Continuing to burden our own shoulders with the guilt of the things we once did is a rejection of the sufficiency of Jesus' atoning work. If you know that you have made a counterfeit virtue of 'perpetual regret', now would be a good time to seek God's forgiveness, so that you may move forward in freedom, with hope and expectancy.

Looking forward with hope

Rueben Job, a retired bishop in the United Methodist Church, observes that 'it is easy to believe we are all trapped into being someone we do not wish to be and living a life we do not desire to live… We fear that there is no way out.' Yet, whatever our childhood influences and regardless of what we may have been told since, we are not passive products of our past. Neither are we doomed to live out a course predetermined for us by others. Job continues, 'To seek help we turn to the One who created us, formed us, and loves us as we are and yet always seeks to lead us to become more than we are' (*Three Simple Rules*, pp. 7–8).

The apostle Peter assures us that God's 'divine power has given us everything we need for life and godliness through our knowledge of him' (2 Peter 1:3). He's writing at a time when ideas about special spiritual knowledge—the possession of only the select few—were gaining ground outside the Church. So he's working hard to make it crystal clear that the only 'knowledge' that counts is available to everyone: it's a full and increasing knowledge to be found by means of a living relationship with Jesus Christ (vv. 2–3, 8). We'll be returning to Peter's summary of how to grow as a Christian but, if you wished, you could read these verses before continuing.

As I've researched and written about spiritual formation, reflected on its course in my own life and observed it in the lives of others, I've become increasingly convinced that those of us who follow Jesus have reason to be hopeful—not in the wishful thinking sense in which the word 'hope' is so often used today, but in the biblical sense of an assured certainty. Personal change is possible: the Bible says so! Paul prayed for the Ephesians that the eyes of their hearts might be enlightened, that they might know the 'extravagance' of God's work in all who trust in him (Ephesians 1:19, *THE MESSAGE*). All who earnestly desire to become more like Christ have the resources of heaven at their disposal. Who could ask for more?

If you sense that you have many features in need of renovation, let me assure you that you're not the first person to feel this way. But it would be good to cultivate the habit of turning your gaze from your own failings to the One who created heaven and earth out of nothing. Is anything too hard for him? Even if your immediate response is 'maybe' or 'yes', keep looking at him and see what happens. Oswald Chambers brings his usual mixture of encouragement and challenge:

*It really is true to say, 'I cannot live a holy life,' but you can decide
to let Jesus Christ make you holy. 'You cannot serve the Lord'—
but you can place yourself in the proper position where God's
almighty power will flow through you. Is your relationship with
God sufficient for you to expect Him to exhibit His wonderful life
in you?*

MY UTMOST FOR HIS HIGHEST, JULY 9

That's a probing question!

If reading this feels too much—if past experiences have
crushed the life out of you, such that stumbling through each
day is enough of a challenge—take heart. 'Looking forward
with hope' is for you, too. Jesus is the one of whom it was
said, 'A bruised reed he will not break, and a smouldering
wick he will not snuff out' (Matthew 12:20, quoting Isaiah
42:3). He fulfils Isaiah's prophetic words describing someone
who would comfort those who mourn, and bestow 'a crown
of beauty instead of ashes, the oil of gladness instead of
mourning, and a garment of praise instead of a spirit of
despair' (Isaiah 61:2–3; see also Luke 4:18–19). You could
start with a simple prayer such as this: 'Jesus, risen Lord
of Life, breathe your life into me.' (I recommend praying it
on waking and last thing at night; at meal times as well, if
you can manage that.) Paul calls our God 'the God of hope'
(Romans 15:13). So you could go on to pray, 'God of hope,
plant and nourish your hope in me.'

In the course of the book, I shall suggest a variety of short
prayers and offer a range of questions to pursue. Rest assured
that I don't expect you to pray or pursue them all one after
the other. The idea is that you listen for God's prompting and

take up those that he highlights for you. (On rereading the book, others may well come to the fore.)

Numerous writers have been used by God to challenge me since I became a Christian in my teens, and I've included quotations from some of them. If the quotations serve to introduce the less well-known among these writers to a wider readership, I shall be delighted; they may also prove useful in the pursuit of areas you feel prompted to explore further. In addition, I've chosen extracts from numerous versions of the Bible. On many occasions, a paraphrased passage has penetrated my heart more deeply than a precise translation; maybe you'll find the same.

Many of the blessings of our lives as followers of Jesus come through sharing the journey with others. My hope is that this book will be used as a way of exploring *together*— for example, in a small group, praying for one another and supporting one another in pressing on. I also hope that what is discovered in the scriptures may in due time be used to raise expectancy about transformation at a church and community level. However, a word of caution…

Starting to think about how best to share what we're learning with others can cause us to refocus—to disengage from hearing God and receiving his grace. Passing on new things from the Lord sounds laudable, but a premature rush to analyse what is being heard in order to teach it may frustrate God's purposes. I have felt it right to describe this rush from hearing to giving out as the spiritual equivalent of bulimia. In so doing I have no wish to trivialise that medical condition: 'spiritual bulimia' is also serious.

When what is taken in is regurgitated before it has had

time to nourish us, there are consequences—not just for the person concerned but also for the body of Christ, which is enfeebled as a result. Those most severely affected appear to have an endless appetite for new things from God but, over time, it becomes clear that his words and his grace have not been internalised: they haven't taken root in the person's heart, where they may grow and bring forth God-glorifying fruit. So, yes, you'll find it valuable to walk this journey in the company of a few others with whom you may share as you go along. But beyond that—well, at least allow God to begin the further work he plans to do in you before stepping back and analysing it for teaching purposes.

As you look forward in hope to God's good plans coming to fruition, you could pray this short prayer: 'Lord, I invite you to renew my heart.'

BIBLE REFLECTIONS

These reflections are designed to be worked through slowly, taking time to hear God speak. He may lead you to come back to a passage—for a day or two, a week or two, or more. Trying to hurry God along doesn't work!

I'm enthusiastic about Eugene Peterson's version of the Bible called THE MESSAGE, not least because it disperses the fog brought by familiarity; I hear God speaking afresh. I shall reproduce passages which I suggest could be read in this version. Reading your usual version alongside will, of course, be valuable. I enjoy using the NIV / THE MESSAGE Parallel Bible (Zondervan, 2004).

1. Read Ephesians 2:1–8 in THE MESSAGE:

It wasn't so long ago that you were mired in that old stagnant life of sin. You let the world, which doesn't know the first thing about living, tell you how to live. You filled your lungs with polluted unbelief, and then exhaled disobedience. We all did it, all of us doing what we felt like doing, when we felt like doing it, all of us in the same boat. It's a wonder God didn't lose his temper and do away with the whole lot of us. Instead, immense in mercy and with an incredible love, he embraced us. He took our sin-dead lives and made us alive in Christ. He did all this on his own, with no help from us! Then he picked us up and set us down in highest heaven in company with Jesus, our Messiah. Now God has us where he wants us, with all the time in this world and the next to shower grace and kindness upon us in Christ Jesus. Saving is all his idea, and all his work. All we do is trust him enough to let him do it. It's God's gift from start to finish!

One way of reflecting on this passage would be to take a sheet of paper (or a page of your journal) and make two columns headed THEN and NOW. Go through the passage, picking out words and phrases to write under whichever heading is appropriate. (There is at least one word that needs to go in both columns.) Those related to the transition between then and now may be written down the middle. Don't hurry: allow God time to speak to you. After all, this isn't school homework to be completed before going out to play.

If aspects of THEN continue to affect you, talk to God about them. Is repentance necessary? If so, be aware of receiving God's forgiveness. Thank God for all that the NOW column, and the transition words, represent. If there are aspects of NOW that have yet to become part of your experience of life as a child of God, talk to him about them and listen to what he says.

2. Read 1 Timothy 4:7b–8.

Focus on the phrase 'train yourself to be godly' ('exercise yourself toward godliness', NKJV) and this question: 'Am I willing to respond by making the choices necessary to live kingdom life now, to the full?' If you're ready to do so, tell God that you're willing for him to direct your steps. Then, as you go about your daily activities, expect him to provide training opportunities.

THE MESSAGE says, 'Exercise daily in God—no spiritual flabbiness, please! Workouts in the gymnasium are useful, but a disciplined life in God is far more so, making you fit both today and forever.' (Discipline and spiritual disciplines are covered in Chapter 5. If the word 'discipline' has negative associations for you, it might be helpful to read those sections now: see pages 126–135.)

3. Read 1 John 3.

'How great is the love the Father has lavished on us, that we should be called children of God! And that is what we are!' (v. 1).

Speak this truth to yourself, out loud if possible, and do

so for as long as seems good to you. If there's no time left to read the whole chapter, so be it. If you're able to read on, do so with your heart, not just your head. There are truths here relating to spiritual heredity and other matters that have already been touched upon. God wants to use them to bless the depths of your heart, not just your intellect. Even if you're not clear about what that last sentence means, it's still possible for the Holy Spirit to be at work in this way, and you could invite him to be so.

1

FOUNDATIONS

At the time of the first draft of this chapter, our second grandchild had been 'in formation' for five months. She had a full complement of organs, some of which had been viewed by means of an ultrasound scan. Nano, as she was known before birth, was reliant on the 'hospitality' of our daughter-in-law, whose dietary choices and routine of rest and exercise were bringing variety to intra-uterine life. As she became increasingly familiar with voices, music and other external sounds, and with the range of responses in her mother's body, this baby was already being formed in ways that went beyond the physical.

Meanwhile, our first grandchild, born to our other son and daughter-in-law, was exploring areas her parents had believed to be out of reach. In her first year, the world beyond the family unit had impacted her in countless ways. For example, legislation had specified safe baby travel equipment for the car bringing her home from the maternity unit; current fashions had influenced some of the gifts she received as a newborn; the city in which she lived had determined the mix of aromas, sights, languages and other sounds bombarding her senses; the weaving of old and newer traditions had made the day of her dedication very special. Imagine how different her formative experiences might have been if she'd been born 100 years earlier.

Then and now

The current enthusiasm for family history has prompted many to research the lives of earlier generations. Most people seem to value the extended sense of continuity. It may also bring insights—for example, why Great-Aunt Agatha was always welcomed so warmly despite her inability to arrive on the correct day, and why Uncle George was unpopular whatever he did. As I've already mentioned, events and attitudes influencing a person, a family or a generation contribute to the shaping of those who come afterwards. If we're committed to becoming more like Jesus and to building God's (one) kingdom, we must be willing to identify legacies from previous generations that are still having an impact. Some we'll be pleased to pass on; others we'll be wanting to bring to a halt before they do even more damage.

Some people feel that growing up was so much easier in 'the good old days', but the reality is that there have always been challenges. Even in the relatively recent past, life expectancy was much shorter than it is today. Less than a century ago, children lost siblings, parents or both to infectious diseases: scarlet fever, polio, tuberculosis and syphilis killed many and enfeebled even more. Wars deprived families of fathers, brothers and uncles; some villages lost all their young men; bombing flattened homes and workplaces. If you've researched your family, you'll probably have come across women who died in childbirth, and maybe also men who died in work-related accidents—both much less common today in the United Kingdom, although, sadly, not everywhere. Are there any signs that beliefs and heart-attitudes formed during such trials have been passed down to your generation?

In years gone by, extended families lived mostly within walking distance. In the absence of welfare benefits and reliable health care, relatives enfolded those who were orphaned or otherwise in need. Yet there have always been children requiring care beyond their family of origin. In his book *The Growth of Love* (BRF, 2008), sociologist and theologian Keith White refers to the residential community Mill Grove, led by successive generations of his family, which has been providing a safe haven for children for more than a century. The continuity of leadership, location and even telephone number has brought a sense of permanence for former residents. Many of them phone or write, decades later, to share news of significant events in their lives or to express concern for other members of the Mill Grove family.

Not all families have a history of faithfulness from which members may draw stability. Family breakdowns, and the practice of moving in with a variety of temporary parent-figures, can leave little ones with wobbly foundations. That's not to say that all such children are irretrievably damaged and, in any case, as I shall emphasise, God is the restorer of foundations. My concern here is to flag up issues that our *laissez-faire* culture might prefer to gloss over.

Childhood in context

I was born in 1949. If that seems an awfully long time ago, be aware that your grandparents, if not your parents, may have a different perspective. And the circumstances I'm about to describe may bring into focus a legacy of your own that needs exploring. In 1949, World War II still coloured many aspects of life, not least because of the longer-term effects on countries and individuals. My father had served in the RAF, taking down messages in Morse code in far-off places and contracting malaria and hepatitis along the way. My mother, who joined the WRNS, had worked as a radio mechanic and driver of lorries. My mother's parents, who lived nearby, had raised two children in the immediate aftermath of World War I. Are you able to identify significant historical markers in the lives of those who brought you up?

I remember visiting our allotment, where fruit and vegetables were grown to supplement the limited range available elsewhere. Apart from the occasion on which I had a close encounter with a gooseberry bush and returned home with prickles in my knees, I remember these as happy times. I was less enthusiastic about the salted runner beans, preserved in Kilner jars in the absence of a freezer. Rationing was soon to end but commodities remained in short supply; radio programmes and newspapers included tales of ingenious ways to 'make do and mend'. 'Waste not, want not' was another maxim of my parents' and grandparents' generations. For some, these maxims contributed to habits of thought and patterns of behaviour that lasted until the day they died, despite changing circumstances. We are to be good stewards of all God gives us, but such sayings may shackle thinking and heart-responding, and be passed down the generations. They may inhibit men and women so that they find it difficult to delight in Father God's loving, gracious, glorious provision for his children; anything more than the absolute minimum somehow feels wrong to them.

In 1938, my mother's family welcomed a 15-year-old Jewish teenager who had arrived alone from Austria; the remaining members of her immediate family died in the Holocaust. Options were few while the war lasted: as an asylum seeker from a hostile country, she was classed as an 'enemy alien'. However, she was permitted to train in child care and, eventually, this provided a springboard into lecturing in education. I knew nothing of this when I was young—only that I enjoyed Lisl's visits and her postcards bearing stamps from foreign parts. Although we're not officially related, she was an influential figure in my early years and remained a much-loved member of our family until her death in 2010.

My mother and her friends also faced school-leaving exams while living with strangers far from home: they were evacuees. As part of the war effort, all girls were taught basic home-making skills. My mother enjoyed recounting the tale of the lady whose advice on hanging out washing was 'Back to the wind when pegging out.' My mother had found a certain dark humour in this phrase, said, as it was, when so many were 'pegging out' in the sense of dying. For bereft adolescents and others, laughter was not just the best but, at times, the only medicine: the National Health Service did not come into being until 1948.

The war-time poster instructing everyone to 'KEEP CALM AND CARRY ON' was never used (it was prepared for extreme circumstances such as enemy invasion) but it sums up the mood of the times very well. Of course, there were also Vera Lynn's bluebirds over the white cliffs of Dover. Vera sang about love and laughter and the longed-for peace. Alongside the austerity, escapist films and optimistic songs had enormous appeal.

Wanting to move on, or recoiling from horrors witnessed, many never spoke of their military experiences. Despite this, for years afterwards, cinema films told high-octane stories of war-time exploits. Similarly, comics for boys included cartoon strips depicting our plucky young servicemen performing heroic acts in defeat of the evil foe. (There was little appetite for anything less cut and dried.) 'Collaborators' were despised; for decades, some people deemed it unpatriotic to buy a car manufactured in Germany or Japan. Those who can't see the point of more recent public acts of repentance aimed at reconciliation must take account of just how deep the enmity was—and the everyday ways in which it was sown into the post-war generation.

Reflecting on the events that shaped those who contributed to my spiritual formation, and on aspects of my childhood, has brought a greater awareness of my foundations and the areas needing renovation. I invite you to take a similar journey. Why not think back to your own beginnings and early years, the people and places that played a part in them, and their historical context? If your grandparents or parents are still alive, consider involving them in the process of remembering, but be aware that no one's memory is totally accurate.

If earlier generations of your family were displaced by war or 'ethnic cleansing' or sought new opportunities through migration, you may already be aware of distinctive attitudes they've passed on. When you recognise important formative influences, you could talk to your heavenly Father about them. If there are big gaps or difficult aspects, it may be freeing to hand them over to him. Whatever the circumstances of your conception and birth, you are 'fearfully and wonderfully made' (Psalm 139:14), and Father God has not taken his eyes off you, even for one second.

However you choose to reflect on your formative years, I have no doubt that God will guide you towards areas of significance. In my experience, this happens through 'chance' conversations or phone calls, items on the news, dreams and in numerous other ways, besides promptings during times of prayer. God is highly creative and endlessly resourceful. The contents of the next section are therefore illustrative rather than an agenda to be followed.

Formative influences

Bear in mind that children are good recorders but poor interpreters: decisions and hardships may have been mis-understood. For example, scarcity of food, having to wear an older sibling's hand-me-downs, being despatched to board-ing school, or the absence of a father travelling for work—these may have been interpreted as demonstrating lack of love or even outright rejection. You could ask God to show you if any inner records need reviewing. If events and their consequences still have pain attached, he is ready to be invited to help with forgiving, receiving healing and moving on.

The way in which a family relates to the outside world can be a pointer to the nature of 'life on the inside'. By this, I don't mean the front the family puts on, although, if the presentation is nothing like the reality, that also speaks volumes. I have in mind the invisible signs posted around family borders. Did yours say WELCOME or KEEP OUT? If the former, who was included in the welcome, and in what range of circumstances? Allowing a small number of people to drink tea from the best china by appointment may have been part of a 'keep out' culture. 'Keep out' warnings may also have applied to God, if he was only spoken of during 'his' hour in church on Sunday.

Families sometimes avoid contact with outsiders because of fear of exposure. Concerns about keeping family secrets may instil deep anxiety in children. Even if they have no idea what the secrets are, the prevailing atmosphere forms them. Abusive relationships of any sort promote secrecy and bring a sense of isolation. For some families, the shame of being in debt leads them to conceal their difficulties: offers of help would feel like the ultimate humiliation. Poverty may also drive people to do things that go against their values. It's sad how many 'good Christian families' live with needs that would be much less burdensome if only they were shared in confidence. Silence robs the body of Christ not only of opportunities to help and support but also of the fully-functioning members that these dear brothers and sisters in Christ could become.

What were the transgenerational conversations like in your family? Were they functional ('Please fetch the milk') or relational? Denigrating ('You'll never be any good at that') or affirming? Distancing ('What do you want *now*? I'm busy') or welcoming? It's not just the words used that communicate: 'How was school today?' said without looking up from the computer or the newspaper, will be received as a mixed message. 'The mouth of a good person is a deep, life-giving well, but the mouth of the wicked is a dark cave of abuse' (Proverbs 10:11, THE MESSAGE). Words, especially from authority figures such as parents and teachers, have great power to build up or to deform, to strengthen or to disable. You could ask God to bring to mind any destructive words that have scarred your inner being. If wounding words were an everyday feature of your childhood, I recommend asking for help as you seek God's cleansing and healing and his renewal of your foundations.

Who were the heroes (real or fictional) of your early years? Can you recall why you felt this way about them at the time? It would be good to consider how men and women you knew or admired as a child, and the institutions you encountered (including the Church), may have influenced your view of the world and what matters in it. Such reflections take time, so be prepared to come back to them for a year or three.

Why not start with those who influenced your view of what it would mean to become an adult? For example, would being an adult mean having the ability to control others, having power over them? Some of us may have learned that being an adult means 'being totally independent and self-sufficient', working all the hours there are, striving to earn enough to be able to say, 'I need no one.' Our understanding of what it means to be grown up not only affects our human relationships but also has consequences for our relationship with God and for our spiritual formation. For example, 'control freakery' (an overwhelming desire to control others), independent-mindedness and self-sufficiency put God at a distance. Long working hours may do the same.

Can you think of influences that shaped your internal picture of what it means to be a Christian (or to be a church-goer, which is, of course, different)? What, if anything, have you grown up expecting to receive from God? God cannot be controlled, and he seeks a relationship with us within which he may care for us as a father cares for a much-loved child. Is there something else written in your heart where those truths should be?

How were masculinity and femininity symbolised to you as you grew up? What do you intuitively 'know' is a man's or a woman's place? Thinking more widely, might you be carrying preformed responses to people of different ethnic or social groups, or set ideas about who is or is not a person worthy of attention? If so, reviewing these ideas in the light of scripture will be a priority. Anxious digging is unnecessary: just ask God to alert you to anything needing attention, and he will do so.

Friends who have ministered for years among those who have grown up under regimes that did not allow freedom of thought or expression have told me of a pervading deadness. This hampers people's responses to God and to one another within the body of Christ. It's the pattern of a 'don't talk; keep out' oppressive family culture multiplied throughout a whole nation. Encouragingly, these friends also have many tales to tell of how God has been able to thaw such frozen landscapes with his love, renewing the foundations of those who have been oppressed and setting them free to serve and bless their nations.

Underpinning the foundations

It's a home-owner's nightmare to discover that the foundations of their house need underpinning—a long and costly process. But it can be done! So what about personal foundations? Philosopher Friedrich Nietzsche is frequently quoted as saying, 'What doesn't kill me makes me stronger' ('*Was mich nicht umbringt, macht mich stärker*'). There's some truth in this statement, but it would be a mistake to try to apply it universally. We are all, to a greater or lesser extent, vulnerable to the shattering effects of trauma, stress and strain, but this is particularly true of the young. Serious trauma at an early age may disable a person for life—and not just physically. Chronic strain (for example, the pressure to grow up too quickly and shoulder inappropriate responsibility) may distort developing foundations.

If our foundations were consolidated higgledy-piggledy years ago, we might assume that we're stuck with what we have. But that would be fatalism. Through God's gracious intervention, those who throughout their adult life have been hampered by a lack of resilience are enabled to press on with a new vigour. I've seen his healing power at work with life-changing results. There are brothers and sisters in Christ who have been specifically called and equipped by God to come alongside those with insecure foundations. Yes, it really is possible for 'places long devastated' to be restored (Isaiah 61:4).

It's worth bearing in mind that when Jesus told the story about the wise man who built his house with proper foundations, and the foolish man who didn't (Luke 6:46–49), he was highlighting the role of adult choices, not childhood experiences—another pointer to our being 'works in progress' rather than irrevocably formed constructions. 'The one who hears my words and does not put them into practice is like a man who built a house on the ground without a foundation. The moment the torrent struck that house, it collapsed and its destruction was complete' (v. 49). It's interesting to note the context of Jesus' story. The specific mindset he was confronting was this: 'Jesus is not to be taken that seriously. You don't have to let what he says change the way you live.' If we're seeking underpinning and strengthening of our foundations, taking what he says seriously will be vital.

A mindset is an attitude with which a person or a people group approaches a situation, and a degree of 'fixedness' is implied. Our mindsets offer clues to the influences that have been forming us. They give shape to the way we think, which affects the way we feel and the way we behave. Over time, all of this solidifies into character. Pessimistic mindsets that say something along the lines of 'No good will come of it, whatever it is' bring mountains of unnecessary pain and suffering into many lives. Such patterns of thinking are, sadly, pretty common, even among Christians, and serve to undermine our trust in God.

Allowing God to renew our minds and choosing to think differently are part of letting him underpin our foundations. They bring no guarantee of changed circumstances, but will most certainly affect our experience. Our mindsets 'flavour' our experience of life; this is one of the reasons why similar experiences may shape individuals in dissimilar ways. There will be another opportunity to review mindsets in Chapter 3 but, for now, why not ask God to bring into consciousness any that are proving a blockage to the work he wants to do, either to renovate your foundations or to bring you into closer fellowship with other members of the body of Christ?

Welcoming God

After all that, where to begin? Jesus said, 'If anyone loves me, he will obey my teaching. My Father will love him, and we will come to him and *make our home with him*' (John 14:23, italics mine). If you're feeling overwhelmed by things to think about, I recommend going back to basics: have you ever told God how welcome he is in your home and in your heart? I've made it a habit to pray, 'Jesus, I welcome you and what you're doing in my life. Holy Spirit, please come and shape the way I think and live.'

Welcoming God himself (not just what he does) is at the heart of spiritual formation and transformation: he is the master builder and the restorer of broken places. How true it is that he can do far more than we are even able to imagine! The prayer below, based on Ephesians 3:14–21 (CJB and NIV), may help you to express trust and hope.

Father, from whom every family in heaven and on earth receives its character, we pray that from the treasures of your glory you will empower us with inner strength by your Spirit, so that Christ may live in our hearts through our trusting. And we pray that, being rooted and founded in love, we and all God's people may be given strength to grasp the breadth, length, height and depth of Christ's love—even though it is beyond all knowing—so that we may be filled with all the fullness of God. Now to you who, by your power working in us, are able to do far beyond anything we can ask or imagine, to you be glory in the Church and in Christ Jesus from generation to generation, for ever and ever! Amen

THE FRUIT OF THE SPIRIT

Love (Greek: *agape*) is first in the list of aspects of the fruit of the Spirit in Galatians 5:22–23, and there's no doubt that it holds first place in other respects as well. Jesus spoke of *agape* love as the distinguishing characteristic by which everyone would identify his disciples (John 13:35). If I don't love, Paul writes, 'I'm nothing but the creaking of a rusty gate... I'm bankrupt without love' (1 Corinthians 13:1, 3, THE MESSAGE).

But there's a problem: beyond the Church, most of what is said, written and sung about love relates to sexual love (*eros*) and to self-gratification. If someone has experienced 'love' only in terms of being used to satisfy the needs of another, they may feel they're better off without it. Within the Church, our understanding of love isn't all it should be, either. Many church communities try hard, but engaging in genuine *agape*-love relationships week in, week out, year after year, is costly. It's tempting to keep things superficial, to walk away when the going gets tough. Let's review the basics before going on to look at love as an aspect of the fruit of the Spirit.

Agape love is a self-giving love which requires nothing in return in order to keep loving. God himself *is* this kind of love (1 John 4:16b): he doesn't just act lovingly, he's Love personified. And the God of love isn't a New Testament discovery. He revealed himself and his love as never before in Jesus, but God's covenant love for his chosen people (more about this in the next chapter) is a thread running through the Old Testament.

If you asked someone to tell you about the Ten Commandments, I wonder how they would characterise them. As a list of 'Don'ts', perhaps? By contrast, Jesus' brief summary centres on the love they call forth: '"Love the Lord your God with all your heart and with all your soul and with all your mind." This is the first and greatest commandment. And the second is like it: "Love your neighbour as yourself." All the Law and the Prophets hang on these two commandments' (Matthew 22:37–40). Jesus fulfilled these commandments in his life and supremely in his death; if you want to know what *agape* love looks like, look at him (see, for example, Romans 5:6–8).

Writing to some of Jesus' first-century apprentices, Paul put it like this:

Watch what God does, and then you do it, like children who learn proper behaviour from their parents. Mostly what God does is love you. Keep company with him and learn a life of love. Observe how Christ loved us. His love was not cautious but extravagant. He didn't love in order to get something from us, but to give everything of himself to us. Love like that.
EPHESIANS 5:1–2 (*The Message*)

It may be helpful to spend a while reflecting on how your concept of love was shaped by your parents and others during your early years. If you sense that something still blocks your understanding of what the scriptures teach about love, why not ask God to set you free?

William Barclay's writing combines a scholarly understanding of the language of the New Testament with a recognition that what we find there is to be lived rather than simply studied. Barclay characterises *agape* love as 'unconquerable benevolence, undefeatable goodwill. *Agape* is the spirit in the heart which will never seek anything but the highest good of its fellow-men. It does not matter how its fellow-men treat it; it does not matter what and who its fellow-men are; it does not matter what their attitude is to it, it will never seek anything but their highest and their best good' (*Flesh and Spirit: an examination of Galatians 5:19–23*, p. 65.)

At the time when Paul's letters were written, contemporary writers considered self-giving love for one or two lovable people to be a noble thing. Yet, speaking to his disciples (a mixed bunch, who didn't always get on), Jesus made it clear that the *agape* love he was looking for was in a different league: 'As the Father has loved me, so have I loved you. Now remain in my love. If you obey my commands, you will remain in my love, just as I have obeyed my Father's commands and remain in his love... My command is this: love each other as I have loved you' (John 15:9–10, 12; see also 17:23).

Jesus says the same to us today. He calls us to love with 'undefeatable goodwill' not only our brothers and sisters in Christ (1 John 4:21) but also our neighbours (Luke 10:25–37) and our enemies (Matthew 5:43–45), and to go on loving those who choose to despise or wound us in return. Impossible? Well, yes and no! We can't love challenging people—or even lots of ordinary people—simply by convincing ourselves that it's a good idea, gritting our teeth and looking for things to like about them. This does not work: in fact, all that teeth-gritting can be a mighty big distraction.

'Love comes from God', writes John (1 John 4:7; see also the following verses). It's possible to love as Jesus did only when we are 'remaining' in him and allowing him to 'remain' in us (John 15:5; see also 17:26). To love as Jesus did, we need his love (an aspect of his essence) residing at the centre of our being. We may welcome him by praying, 'God who is Love, come, be love in me.' Then, one day, we'll be able to look back in thankfulness as we see how the love of God, poured into our hearts by the Holy Spirit (Romans 5:5), has been overflowing to others. Over time, by God's grace, the fruit of his Spirit will become evident. Therein lies our only hope of being able to love as Jesus did.

Mother Teresa is often quoted as having said that the worst disease in the world today is not tuberculosis or leprosy but the poverty born of a lack of love. If we have unstable foundations (not grounded in love), we may find it hard not only to give and receive love in relationships in general, but also to grasp the magnitude of God's love for us. He is love: remember, this is not simply what he does; it's what he is through and through. And it's what he is in relation to us— to me, to you, personally—not just in relation to others or to people in general.

If you know you have a tendency to edit out words about God's love for you, why not pause to hear what he wants to say before continuing? If you know that you struggle in this way (or even if you don't), you could make this a daily prayer: 'Father, please enlarge my heart's capacity to receive love from you and from others.' Don't let anyone tell you that praying for yourself in this way is selfish. It's inviting God to go on restoring you to be the person he created you to be. In due time, this will enable you to live out your calling to love others, and to delight his Father-heart as you do so. 'There's my dear child, _____ , growing more like Father every day!' (Put your name in the space.)

BIBLE REFLECTIONS

1. Read Mark 10:13–16.

Note the different groups of people mentioned in this account. With which group do you identify most strongly—those bringing children to Jesus, the children being brought, the disciples who still lacked understanding of Jesus and his ways? Notice Jesus' response to each of the groups. Visualise Jesus sitting on a grassy bank, welcoming a group of small children, including you. If you are able, sit with Jesus for a moment and receive his blessing.

Much-loved child of God, what would you like to say to him? Is there anything he wants to say to you?

2. Read Proverbs 22:6.

'Train a child in the way he should go, and when he is old he will not turn from it.' Memorise this verse and take it with you into your day. Call it to mind at work, at home and when travelling, as you tackle the various jobs to be done and relate to people in a range of situations. Ask Father God to highlight where helpful or unhelpful patterns of living or relating were set down in your childhood. How may these patterns have contributed to the formation of your character? Are they already influencing members of the next generation? Bring before God what you discover, and listen for his response.

3. Read 1 Corinthians 13.

This passage paints a picture of the *agape* love of Father God being expressed in the lives of his children. It complements Paul's description of the fruit of the Spirit in Galatians 5:22 and 23: with God's love deep in our inner being, what comes out will be not only love but also patience, kindness and so on.

Take a sheet of paper (or turn to a new page in your journal) and write the characteristics of love as found in 1 Corinthians 13 down the left-hand side. Then, alongside each one, make a note from the relevant verse in Galatians. Add anything you're aware of the Lord saying to you about these characteristics. Is there one in particular that you sense he is wanting to form in you at the moment?

2

LEARNING TO TRUST

When we trust, we choose to rely upon the ability or integrity of a person or group. Trust provides a basis for thoughts, decisions and actions, and comes into play particularly when there's an element of risk. Trust, or lack of it, will affect how we feel, but trust is not an emotion. The situation may be pretty straightforward, such as 'Do I trust this carrier to deliver this parcel in time for my friend's birthday?' or as complicated as 'Do I trust this man who says he wants to marry my daughter?'

When Jesus asked, 'Which of you fathers, if your son asks for a fish, will give him a snake instead? Or if he asks for an egg, will give him a scorpion?' (Luke 11:11–12) he clearly wasn't expecting anyone to say, 'Well, I would!' Jesus' focus was the goodness of God—the 'how much more' of the goodness of our heavenly Father. Yet his question and assumed response also point to God's plan that human families (extended families, not just parents and children) should be nurturing, life-imparting places. God's will is that, within families, children may experience trustworthiness and committed, loving provision, and be formed into adults with the capacity to care not only for the next generation but also for each other.

Keith White emphasises the vital role of the local community in the development of children, and mentions it specifically in relation to their understanding of the making and keeping of promises. He asks, if children grow up in settings in which there is 'no experience of promises that are made and kept, how will they acquire the idea of relationships that transcend crises, disagreements and adversity, sickness, health, competing attentions and attractions, old age, weariness and poverty? False promises are like slugs and poison in the social compost of the young child's early years.' He adds that 'politicians and professional footballers will regularly renege on their manifesto promises or contracts in the light of "events"'. Somewhere in the community 'there must be those who demonstrate genuine covenant' (*The Growth of Love*, pp. 201–202).

People of God, are we ready and able to stand in this crucial gap? You may find it helpful to reflect on your own early experiences of trustworthiness and promise-keeping, and on their contribution to your internal framework.

When a child's trust is betrayed, it may have far-reaching consequences for his or her life and future relationships. Some will internalise a distorted picture of God, assuming that because he's called 'Father' he's like the dad who abandoned them or the Reverend Father who abused them. Those betrayed as children are likely to find that learning to trust God (and his people) takes a very long time. If you know that this applies to you, it would be good to invite Jesus to walk alongside you through what follows. He is full of grace and truth. If you ask him, he will help you build a more accurate picture of Father God and gently highlight areas in which internalised distortions continue to have an effect. If painful memories emerge, it's safe to talk to God about them—and he can hear your heart's cry if you can't find the words. You may also find it helpful to share the memories with a friend or counsellor.

Even those whose experience of family life has left them scarred and wary can often think of one person who stood out as different: someone who cared without suffocating or demanding an inappropriate response; someone who taught them that healthy love could be for them, too. Just one person demonstrating loving consistency may be sufficient to give a child the foundations for personal resilience and a sense of self, allowing them to develop the capacity to trust. Thinking back, is there a particular person (in your family or wider community) whose caring commitment to you during your early years or whose steadying support in a time of crisis remains memorable? If so, how about taking a moment to thank God for that person?

Belief and trust in God

When surveyed, many people in the UK say they believe in God, but what do they mean by 'believe in'? Do they mean that, on balance, they think God probably does exist, or more than that? The English words 'belief' and 'faith' have become disconnected from their biblical meaning. For many people today, faith means little more than a tick in a box on a form, vaguely linked to a set of ideas, sometimes ill-defined and little understood. The motto 'In God we trust' has appeared on US currency since 1864, but how many on either side of the Atlantic see trusting God day by day as a logical consequence of belief? Such has been the drift that, these days, anyone who lives a life shaped by their religious beliefs risks being seen as a 'fundamentalist'—which the media seem to equate with being weird, maybe even dangerous.

In his *Jewish New Testament Commentary*, David Stern writes about the Greek New Testament word *pistis*, commonly translated as 'faith'. He explains that in most instances he prefers to use the word 'trust', as this 'more clearly signifies to English-speakers the confident reliance on God that generates holy deeds, as opposed to mere mental acknowledgment of facts and ideas' (p. 229). In Stern's translation, the Complete Jewish Bible, Hebrews 11 begins, 'Trusting is being confident of what we hope for, convinced about things we do not see' and continues to put 'by trusting' in each verse where 'by faith' appears in most other versions. Why not try reading Hebrews 11 to yourself, making this substitution?

There's a verse of scripture which, in many versions, speaks of walking or living by faith, not by sight. If this verse is well known to you, it may be instructive to call to mind the images and thought-patterns you associate with it. Stern's version says, 'For we live by trust, not by what we see' (2 Corinthians 5:7, CJB). Which words or phrases might you use to express to a friend your understanding of living by trust? Are you aware of having moved beyond 'mental acknowledgment' to a relationship with a trustworthy heavenly Father, and a reliance upon him that 'generates holy deeds'?

Trusting enough to follow and keep following

I shall refer more extensively to Paul Bradbury's book, *Life from Death Emerging*, in the next chapter, but a point he makes is relevant here. He writes of the need to allow ourselves to believe in the omnipotence and compassionate heart of God, without our belief becoming conditional on his demonstrating that power and compassion by doing what we have asked him to do. In a consumer culture that encourages us to abandon a service provider whenever someone else promises a better deal, a trust in God that has to be learned, developed and strengthened by way of ups and downs over time seems so… well, slow.

In the New Testament, the call to trust and follow comes from Jesus himself. As his earthly ministry moved towards its climax, he spelled out the non-negotiable terms to his closest friends: 'Anyone who intends to come with me has to let me lead. You're not in the driver's seat; *I* am' (Matthew 16:24, THE MESSAGE). Dietrich Bonhoeffer emphasised that if we follow someone, it means we don't know where we're going, adding: 'When we are called to follow Christ, we are summoned to an exclusive attachment to his person… Christ calls, the disciple follows; that is grace and commandment in one' (*The Cost of Discipleship*, p. 16. This book, first published in 1937, was originally entitled *Nachfolge*. The word lacks an exact English equivalent but has the sense of 'following after' or 'succession'). For Bonhoeffer, following Christ brought conflict with the Nazis in Germany even before the start of World War II. On 9 April 1945, he was executed at Flossenburg concentration camp. You could ask yourself, 'Am I prepared to keep on following when I don't know where I'm going—or when I fear that I *do* know?'

Practising following in quieter times may serve as a preparation for periods of turbulence, but it is also true that daily faithfulness in small things has inherent value. Oswald Chambers wrote, 'If I obey Jesus Christ in the seemingly random circumstances of life, they become pinholes through which I see the face of God' (*My Utmost for His Highest*, November 2). What an inspiring picture! How about praying that today you'll know more of the reality it represents?

Different personalities find different aspects of discipleship more or less of a struggle. For example, those who delight in variety and welcome the unexpected may find weeks when the Lord is asking them to keep pressing on in the same direction—and nothing seems to be changing—a hard grind. The test for them is whether they are able to remember their commitment to trust and follow at the point where they might otherwise wander off in search of something more interesting. On the other hand, I, along with many others, prefer orderliness. Guess which aspects of following we find most challenging!

Our culture applauds self-sufficient activism and often equates delay with wasted time. A trusting relationship with God will enable us not only to act decisively when so led, but also to wait for his direction, to go on waiting when all around are clamouring, 'Don't just stand there, do something!' Trusting God will also influence our perspective on the big picture, from ancient history to eternity. Even so, an untroubled existence is unlikely: from humankind's earliest days, there have been whispers along the lines of, 'Did God really say...?' (Genesis 3:1). So, *is* God to be trusted? Whatever our personal experience (and some, overwhelmed by pain or disappointment or by difficulties affecting those they love, have concluded that the answer is 'No'), God's track record over thousands of years points towards the answer 'Yes'.

A covenant-keeping God

The covenant faithfulness of God is a recurring theme in the Old Testament. If you struggle with trusting in general or with trusting God in particular, taking time to study this theme will be immensely rewarding. I find it encouraging that, after it is recorded that 'Abram believed the Lord, and he credited it to him as righteousness', Abram felt able to ask God how he would know that God's promises were to be fulfilled (Genesis 15:6, 8). God responded not with a 'try harder to believe' pep-talk but with a dramatic demonstration of his deep and everlasting commitment to Abram. God gave his assurance through the ancient symbolism of a covenant ceremony (vv. 9–21), knowing that this would speak the truth of his commitment deep into Abram's heart. In those days, no one—but *no one*—broke covenant.

Marriage services today include symbolic acts, such as an exchange of rings and a joining of hands, to emphasise the covenant nature of the commitment being entered into. Similarly, in ancient covenant ceremonies, the parties used traditional means of symbolising their coming together in an indissoluble agreement. One was an exchange of names. When God made the covenant with Abram, the latter became known as Abraham (17:5). God was happy to be known as 'the God of Abraham' and later as 'the God of Abraham, Isaac and Jacob' (see Exodus 3:6; Matthew 22:32). These patriarchs occupy a special place in the history of God's people but, if you're in a covenant relationship with him today, he is pleased also to be known as 'the God of _____' (put your name here). God's commitment to his people is not only to them as a group; it's also intensely personal. If this idea is new to you, why not take a moment to allow it to sink in?

God's covenant love is often expressed by use of the Hebrew word *hesed*, also translated as loving-kindness, faithfulness, mercy, grace or goodness. The Psalms provide many opportunities to mine the depth and breadth of meaning in this word, with translators employing a variety of expressions in an attempt to do it justice. For example, the King James Bible renders the beginning of Psalm 31:7, 'I will be glad and rejoice in thy mercy', while the Good News Bible refers to God's 'constant love'. THE MESSAGE paints a word-picture designed to convey something of the joy and security brought by God's covenant love: 'I'm leaping and singing in the circle of your love.' I hear echoes of this in the advice given in Jude 21, which the Living Bible translates, 'Stay always within the boundaries where God's love can reach and bless you.'

In their finer moments, the Old Testament people of God didn't just tell one another, 'Our God is faithful'; they lived and journeyed with that knowledge as a glorious, life-enhancing, unassailable reality at the core of their community. It was the rock under their feet, the foundation for their everyday lives, their hope for future generations, and a good reason to sing, feast and generally celebrate. Hallelujah! In less worthy moments, though, they forgot all about it and panicked, putting their trust in unholy alliances with whoever was willing to promise protection at the time. Some of the conflicts troubling the world right now are a consequence of such hasty misalliances, ancient and modern. You could ask God to alert you if an unholy alliance ever starts to look like the way out of a dilemma of your own.

Worrying versus expectant trust

'The name of the Lord is a strong tower; the righteous run to it and are safe' (Proverbs 18:10); 'The Lord is my shepherd, I shall not be in want' (Psalm 23:1); 'I am with you always' (Jesus' promise in Matthew 28:20). We may be familiar with the words, but some of us know that we haven't allowed these, and the vast number of other reassuring Bible verses and passages, to shape our thinking and penetrate our 'worry-guts'. In fact, if worrying were a sport, we'd be in demand by all the top teams.

Anxiety has many causes. It may be a response to a crisis, a consequence of unhealed trauma or a symptom of physical or mental illness. Whatever the cause, mental habits can perpetuate anxiety. If we practise worrying for several hours each day—even practising in the middle of the night—no wonder we're so good at it! In the Sermon on the Mount, Jesus queried why children of a gracious heavenly Father were pursuing this fruitless activity (Matthew 6:25–34). If Jesus were to ask the same question today, how would you respond?

Commenting on Jesus' words, 'Do not worry about your life' (v. 25), Chambers notes, 'Jesus did not say that the person who takes no thought for anything in his life is blessed— no, that person is a fool. But Jesus *did* teach that His disciple must make his relationship with God the dominating focus of his life, and to be cautiously carefree about everything else in comparison to that' (*My Utmost for His Highest*, May 21). By way of illustration, Jesus' friends were unable to comprehend how he could sleep peacefully in the stern of the boat while the storm raged (Mark 4:38), but of course they'd had more practice at panicking and a lot less practice at trusting than he had.

Worrying undermines the development of trust and smothers *shalom* peace. It has been called 'practical atheism'. By contrast, the attitude of mind that I have called 'expectant trust' makes our hearts fertile ground within which God-given peace may take root and flourish. Paul advised the Colossians, 'Let the *shalom* which comes from the Messiah be your heart's decision-maker' (Colossians 3:15, CJB). Which of the words or phrases in the last four paragraphs best describes your way of approaching life?

The apostle Paul chose expectant trust as his way of life. The night after he'd been called to account by the Jewish leaders and caused a terrible uproar, the Lord appeared to him and said, 'Take courage! As you have testified about me in Jerusalem, so you must also testify in Rome' (Acts 23:11). Despite life-threatening conspiracy, shipwreck and official inertia, Paul lived to do just that (28:17–30). God's commission to speak for him in Rome will have sustained Paul when Governor Felix chose to adjourn his case for the umpteenth time (24:22–26). Two years later, when a violent storm at sea appeared to be about to take Paul and everyone on board ship to a watery grave, God sent an angel to reinforce his message (27:23–24). By God's grace, all survived. Paul's trust was instrumental: he urged everyone to eat something in order to have the strength to reach the shore (vv. 34–36). Imagine the possible outcome if God's man on the spot had been looking at the waves and panicking along with the rest of them, rather than living by trust.

Bible teacher and author Guy Chevreau frequently prays, and encourages others to pray, 'Father, I receive the grace You have for me this day.' While working on material for a book, Chevreau's laptop bag was stolen from his host's van. He explains, 'I lost not only my computer, but my digital camera, my iPod and headphones, several hundred dollars of cash, my passport and all my ID' (*Vital Signs of a Healthy Church*, p. 27). A long way from home, standing amid the broken glass from the van window, he repeated the grace-receiving prayer several times.

Chevreau comments that, alongside the sufferings of those whose loved ones have been martyred for their faith, the theft of his personal belongings was 'trivial, inconvenient at worst. Nevertheless,' he adds, 'it could have spun my little world out of orbit.' In the heat of a highly charged moment, the prayer was a way of expressing the 'unshakeable confidence' he had, and that we also may have, that God is for us and not against us. Chevreau writes, 'In spite of desperate circumstances it is ours to trust that God is nevertheless working larger kingdom purposes in the midst of things. After we'd finished with the police report, I looked out over a beautiful Surrey valley and said out loud, "Lord, I'm really looking forward to seeing how You're going to redeem this mess"' (p. 27).

If you know that the word 'worry-guts' describes you or that your world is easily spun out of orbit, how about trying an experiment? Memorise as much of Psalm 23 as you can over the next few days. When you notice that you're becoming anxious, spend two minutes focusing your attention on the verses learned so far. If you're awake in the middle of the night, thoughts a-whirling, call the verses to mind again. Then allow the Lord's Prayer to draw your thoughts towards the Father and his will being done. (So far, praying the Lord's Prayer during the night has not kept me awake! I find this more constructive than praying through my concerns in the night, unless I have a specific prompting to pray.)

Blockages to God's grace

There's a trio of grace-defying stances that I've called 'The Three Dys-graces', the first of which is self-protection. The other two are self-justification and self-pity. If you would welcome examples of how such stances may impact a relationship with God, have a look at Genesis 3 and 4.

Many of my generation were taught as children to say, 'Sticks and stones may break my bones, but words will never hurt me.' The adult equivalent, the legendary British stiff upper lip epitomised by 'keeping calm and carrying on', can help people to keep going in appalling circumstances. That's why, in some quarters, it's seen as laudable. However, over time, it predisposes to an unhealthy handling of emotions. Even more seriously, the associated tendency to exclude potential helpers (including God) also serves as a barrier to grace. If you have been brought up to live life this way, you may need to talk to God about it before reading further. You could ask him if there's pride or self-sufficiency to be repented of, or if old wounds need healing.

We're vulnerable to developing self-protection strategies as we grow up. 'How was your day at school, dear?' 'Fine, Mum,' we say, to avoid interrogation about overdue homework or playground bullying; we've already suffered enough at the hands of teachers or others at school. Some of us learn to opt out of friendships whenever they start to become close: 'I'll reject you before you reject me, because that way I'll feel in control, and it will hurt less.' If, decades later, we're still saying 'Fine', regardless of the truth, and pushing everyone away, we have chosen a rocky road.

Self-protection strategies may be passed down the generations, even in families where God is known. Can you see how you may have been influenced during your childhood and adolescence by the way others handled crises? Some anxious parents teach their children to 'protect' themselves by always imagining the worst and 'expecting' it to be the outcome. If there's no disaster, they're laughing; if their worst fears materialise, there's a perverted sense of control in being right.

Those who learned at an early age that it was dangerous to trust anyone may choose self-protection, secretly vowing, 'Never again...'. Even as adults, they may continue to protect themselves from the sense of vulnerability that trusting can bring, thus making close relationships—loving and being loved—very difficult. This approach is common not only among those who have been abused but also among those who have felt abandoned when a parent has died. It's also found where there has been significant emotional abandonment— for example, due to parental preoccupation with work (paid or voluntary) or another all-consuming activity. The effective absence of a parent from their role on account of mental health problems, alcoholism, drug addiction and so on, also predisposes a child to self-protection.

Self-protection strategies are barriers to expectant trust, and God's children need to be prepared to repent of and relinquish them. The good news is that, by God's grace, these strategies may be unlearned. Asking your heavenly Father to alert you when you're next about to act in this way could enable you to welcome his grace instead of swinging into self-protection mode.

By way of clarification: God-honouring self-care is not the issue under consideration here. We are to be good stewards of all that God has entrusted to us, including our bodies and minds. Self-care will include eating a sensible diet; taking an appropriate amount of time off to recover after medical treatment; allowing others to share the burdens in the days surrounding a bereavement; booking time with friends who refresh, encourage and generally bless us; not allowing demands for new budget calculations (or whatever is pressing in) to dictate the speed of swallowing food... I could go on, but I hope you can already see what I mean. If not, ask God to highlight any self-care issues in your own life. God-honouring self-care is part of the responsibility God entrusts to us. By contrast, ungodly self-protection is usurping God's responsibility—not allowing our heavenly Father, our covenant-keeping faithful God, to do and be all that he has promised to do and be.

Let's move on to consider self-justification. Jesus discerned this in the hearts of some Pharisees who sneered at him (Luke 16:14–15). It was also behind the law expert's question that prompted the story of the good Samaritan (10:29). I know from my own experience that it's possible to self-justify silently. Whether shared or kept to ourselves, self-justification is highly effective in distancing us from God and from others. Bonhoeffer warned that 'self-justification and judging others go together, as justification by grace and serving others go together' (*Life Together*, p. 70). In much of today's media-driven world, such behaviour passes for normal, so it's worth asking God to raise our awareness of it.

Self-pity says, 'Poor me!' (and usually a lot more besides) in an internal monologue, which may include implicit or explicit criticism of God or others. Whatever the content, it drowns out God's voice, thereby becoming gloomily self-fulfilling: blocking input from God does tend to make things worse. Self-pitying words and body-language draw others in, especially those of a caring disposition.

Men and women who train as counsellors learn how to listen to the pain and distress of others in a caring way without joining them 'on the pity pot'. This skill needs to be more widely taught within the body of Christ! The key is to stay anchored on truth and grace, while asking the Holy Spirit to show how best to help the self-pitying friend to look up and out of their distress. Refocusing will allow the person to discern what is real and needs facing (for example, a relationship difficulty or mounting debts) and to go on to hear what God is saying about it. The best sort of help does three things: it communicates acceptance of the person without buying in to their distorted perceptions, it reinforces the truth that they are loved and valued, and it reminds them of the goodness and faithfulness of God.

Remembering together

Memory keeps me connected to who I am and to my personal journey. It also links me to those with whom I have shared experiences, and to earlier generations through the memories of others. When families get together and relax, they may play, 'Do you remember when...?' Telling and retelling stories about people and events, and sharing them with new members, increases the sense of cohesiveness not only in families but also in villages and other communities.

When written texts were rare, conversations within the family and the community of God's people were an indispensable way of bringing to mind important truths, while at the same time passing them on. For example, Moses urged parents to go through the Lord God's commandments with their children, and to talk about them at home, when out and about, at bedtime and on getting up in the morning (Deuteronomy 6:7). These days, we're spoiled for choice when it comes to methods of recording beliefs and values and of communicating them to the next generation. None the less, first-hand personal testimony and community stories of what God has done are still precious reminders of what he's like, what he can do and what we're part of.

Honouring God's faithfulness from generation to generation helps to build trust in him, so church communities with a sense of expectancy and a desire to move on with God need to make sure they're not so future-focused that they edit out the past. Yes, it's heartening to know that God is alive and has been active today in our neighbourhood and the wider world. But it's also good to hear stories of his faithfulness over time, not only from scripture but also from older church members who committed themselves to following Christ decades ago. (Some choose to keep a journal, a valuable reminder of his responses to prayers and other experiences of his faithfulness.) If you've been a Christian for years, what would you say to a new disciple who asked how being able to trust God has shaped the person you've become?

Thinking about your church community and asking the same question, are you able to see how 'trusting the Lord' and 'leaning not on your own understanding' (Proverbs 3:5) have shaped your corporate life? What testimony do you have to the faithfulness of God at times of financial pressure, shared grief or disappointment? It's essential to address such questions at a corporate level because, whatever your intentions, the answers and the realities behind them are already shaping the members, especially the younger ones, and, through them, affecting the wider community. If our evangelism paints a picture of a trustworthy God, this same trust must be evident in the way church business and leadership meetings are conducted. Otherwise, people will become confused and will be shaped by the incongruity (teaching one thing and living another), rather than by learning to trust God.

Before leaving the subject of remembering, have you noticed how many times in the Bible God's people were instructed or inspired to put in place a pattern of remembrance? One of the reasons for this will have been the need to keep in mind the bigger picture—the story of God's never-ending *hesed* love down the centuries. Here are a few examples of remembrances. The Passover (Deuteronomy 16:1) and Purim

(Esther 9:28) were instituted to bring to mind specific acts of deliverance. The remembrance of his death through broken bread and poured-out wine that Christ instituted (Luke 22:19–20) is inextricably linked with the deeply symbolic Seder (Passover) meal eaten at home by Jewish families once a year. Paul commended remembrance of the new covenant to the church in Corinth (1 Corinthians 11:23–26). Today, Christmas, Easter and Pentecost provide opportunities for us to retell the story of God's saving grace for all and his empowering of his people, and to receive afresh from him. I sympathise with those who are minded to dispense with Christmas on account of its secularisation, but each year I still look forward to it. I set my heart to welcome again the 'good news of great joy' and invite Immanuel, God with us, to make his presence known and felt. It always ends up being such a blessing.

Seeing—or not?

Since my early days as a follower of Jesus, I've been familiar with Bible verses about trusting God. More recently, I've appreciated that I can only truly say I'm trusting him when I don't understand what he's doing—when my 'faith' is taking me further ahead than my 'sight' can see. Looking back, it seems such an elementary lesson! Why did it take so long to learn?

I've also come to accept that when God appears to be doing nothing in response to prayers prayed in faith, it's entirely possible that he's at work in ways I can't yet see—or may never see. Becoming more aware of God and his behind-the-scenes activities, I've adjusted to the fact that my inability to see isn't the big deal I used to think it was. Yes, by God's grace it is possible to 'live by trust, not by what we see' (2 Corinthians 5:7, CJB). With the wisdom of hindsight, I know that this has been a vitally important building block in my spiritual formation, for which I thank God. If you also would welcome a greater trust in God, you could pray this prayer: 'Father, please expand my heart's capacity to trust.'

THE FRUIT OF THE SPIRIT

Continuing to look at the fruit of the Spirit, the character of Christ being formed in us, we now come to joy and peace. Jesus mentioned them, alongside *agape* love, in his final briefing to his followers (John 14—16). They were about to face testing beyond anything they had previously experienced, and Jesus wanted to strengthen their trust in him. Which points did he labour?

Jesus offered several explanations of why he said what he did that evening. For example, 'I've told you these things for a purpose: that my joy might be your joy, and your joy wholly mature... I've told you all this so that trusting me, you will be unshakable and assured, deeply at peace' (John 15:11; 16:33, THE MESSAGE). If you are able, read these chapters now, noting some things Jesus said that might have enabled his disciples to receive his joy and peace in the calm before the storm.

The word 'joy' is sometimes used interchangeably with 'happiness', but the latter so often deserts us when we don't get our way or when trouble strikes. True joy is deeper and less vulnerable to circumstances. Joy acts as a spiritual disinfectant, preventing uncharitable attitudes from taking up residence; it's impossible to be resentful, envious or bitter while filled with joy. The joy planted and watered by the work of the Spirit of Jesus in believers' hearts also contributes to their resilience. No doubt that's one of the reasons Jesus wanted his friends to receive his joy before his crucifixion. Hundreds of years before, Nehemiah had said to God's people, 'The joy of the Lord is your strength' (Nehemiah 8:10). In the centuries since, so many brothers and sisters in Christ who have been oppressed, imprisoned and martyred for their faith have lived the truth of these words, to the amazement of those trying to break their spirits.

C.S. Lewis was an atheist for half of his life. The story of his journey from atheism to faith in Christ is chronicled in his autobiography, *Surprised by Joy*. Lewis is sometimes quoted as describing joy as 'the serious business of Heaven'—which could appear to imply that he visualised heavenly joy as sober rather than exuberant. Far from it! The words 'serious business' refer not to the mood but to the sense of purpose and intent in being occupied with joy in heaven. We think of the making merry enjoyed in our earthly time off as frivolous, Lewis observed, but 'everything is upside down' in this world (*Letters to Malcolm: Chiefly on Prayer*, p. 122).

At numerous points in *The Chronicles of Narnia*, Lewis' characters have experiences of joy which, in our upside-down world, could be dismissed as childish. Many of my generation learned as children not to be too demonstrative; for example, it was 'silly' to jump for joy. If you've been moulded by such restrictions, it's time to seek release. Some followers of Jesus speak loyally of their joy in the Lord as a matter of faith, yet with little or no heart-experience. If this describes you, why not ask God about it? Welcome Jesus, the Lord of Joy, 'who for the joy set before him endured the cross' (Hebrews 12:2). Invite his Spirit to form this aspect of his character in you, and revel in a foretaste of heaven. You could enjoy *The Chronicles of Narnia* while you're waiting!

The English word 'peace' may be used to refer to a remedy for inner turmoil or untidy emotions, or peace for a conflict-ridden world. Others speak of 'peace and quiet'—meaning withdrawal to a spot well away from demanding people. However, behind the word 'peace' in the New Testament (Greek: *eirene*), and hence important for understanding its meaning in this context, lies the rich Hebrew word *shalom*. Although also translated 'peace', *shalom* comes from a very different mindset and, rather than making assumptions based on the English word, we must listen carefully to its different range of notes and harmonies. *Shalom* is essentially God-focused (see, for example, Paul's assertion that 'the mind controlled by the Spirit is life and peace', Romans 8:6). Whereas false peace blankets over emotions and difficulties, *shalom* speaks of wholeness, of the well-being of lives lived in the safe care and nurture of a God who can be trusted, and of divine order permeating every aspect of life.

Around the time of the setting up and dedication of the tabernacle (which signified the presence of God with his people in the wilderness), the Lord told Moses that Aaron and his sons were to use a particular form of priestly blessing. You've probably heard it: it's still used in many churches today. These words speak more effectively to my heart than any dictionary definition of peace:

The Lord bless you and keep you;
the Lord make his face shine upon you and be gracious to you;
the Lord turn his face toward you and give you [shalom] peace.
NUMBERS 6:24–26

The same *shalom*-infused, Father-focused well-being is seen in Jesus—and not just when everything around him is quiet and well-ordered. Picture Jesus, knowing God the Father's eye lovingly upon him, offering his peace to those remaining after Judas has gone out to betray him (John 14:27; 16:33). Jesus tells them not to let their hearts be troubled, not to be afraid (14:27). He knows what's about to happen but he still has peace, and he is inviting others to receive that same peace. It's a peace rooted in trust, not in denial or avoidance. Might recalling this picture of Jesus at peace, and taking time to welcome his peace, be helpful in your current circumstances?

Writing from prison to the Christians at Philippi, Paul exhorted them to 'rejoice in the Lord always' and not to be anxious; to allow God's peace to guard their hearts and minds in Christ Jesus (Philippians 4:4, 6–9). THE MESSAGE version of this well-known passage reads like this:

Celebrate God all day, every day. I mean, revel in him! … Let petitions and praises shape your worries into prayers, letting God know your concerns. Before you know it, a sense of God's whole-ness, everything coming together for good, will come and settle you down. It's wonderful what happens when Christ displaces worry at the centre of your life. Summing it all up, friends, I'd say you'll do best by filling your minds and meditating on things true, noble, reputable, authentic, compelling, gracious—the best, not the worst; the beautiful, not the ugly; things to praise, not things to curse. Put into practice what you learned from me, what you heard and saw and realised. Do that, and God, who makes everything work together, will work you into his most excellent harmonies.

Centuries earlier, Isaiah had pointed to the relationship between trust in God and peace: 'You will keep in perfect peace him whose mind is steadfast ['stayed on thee', KJV], because he trusts in you' (Isaiah 26:3). We have a choice: we can focus on the troubles about which we fear we can do nothing, and allow our trust in God to be undermined and our peace disturbed, or we can look to Jesus, choosing to trust despite turbulent emotions while his peace takes root and grows in our hearts. If you know you have a tendency to take the former approach, why not ask God to enlarge your capacity to receive his Spirit and the *shalom* peace he brings?

Thinking more widely, are you aware of areas in the life of your extended family or community that are currently providing fertile soil for the roots of resentment or a joyless bitterness—perhaps areas in which trust has been betrayed? If you are ready to do so, ask God to show you how he wants to work through you to bring *shalom*, healing and hope. We may all pray, 'God of hope, fill us with all joy and peace as we trust in you, so that we may overflow with hope by the power of the Holy Spirit' (based on Romans 15:13).

BIBLE REFLECTIONS

It's vital to consider issues of trust before going on to look at the formative effect of adversity. In the absence of trust (specifically, trust in God) adversity may crush us.

1. Read 2 Corinthians 1:8–11.

Paul wanted the Christians in Corinth to know how he had faced and endured unspecified difficulties in Asia. Why do you think this was so? Think back to what you have read about the expectant trust he showed over many years. Imagine its effect on those around him: non-believers and followers of Jesus, especially those facing persecution. Elsewhere he wrote, 'Whatever you have learned or received or heard from me, or seen in me—put it into practice. And the God of peace will be with you' (Philippians 4:9). Ask God what he wants to teach you through reflecting on the ripple effect of Paul's trust. Keep open this dialogue as you go about your activities today, and see what the Lord highlights for you.

2. Read 2 Kings 6:8–17.

At a particularly difficult time, this passage became a source of inspiration for me. Try reading it slowly, putting yourself in the place of Elisha's servant and then of Elisha. Ask God if there's something he wants to teach you through it. If there are seemingly overwhelming challenges in your present circumstances, you could pray, 'O Lord, open my eyes so that I may see', asking God to reveal where he is at work in unseen ways.

3. Read Philippians 4:4–9.

Paul encouraged Jesus' followers at Philippi to fill their minds with good things. Adopting this approach will affect not only how we view God and life but also our ability to receive God's *shalom*. This reading could be the basis for a practical exercise: ask the Lord to direct your eyes to what is right, pure, lovely, admirable, excellent and praiseworthy in situations you come across, even if they also have more difficult aspects. Then celebrate in your heart what is good, sharing your observations or celebrations with others if appropriate. (This exercise does *not* require you to turn a blind eye to sin that needs confronting, or to call grey 'colourful' in order to sound more positive!)

3

THE SCHOOL OF ADVERSITY

Definitions of 'adversity' include words such as opposition, misfortune, distress, difficult circumstances, hard knocks and affliction. Of course, one person's minor hiccup may be another's total disaster. I tried to teach my children the difference between their 'anguish' due to delayed gratification (having to wait for what they wanted) and true suffering (such as that experienced by those with nothing to eat for days on end). It's good to remind ourselves—and maybe one another, too—that being sneered at by colleagues for our faith is a world away from the horrific adversities suffered by brothers and sisters in Christ elsewhere. And, in an age in which compensation is increasingly sought for minor hurts, we do well to remember that litigation is not the only possible response to offences against us.

When we're 'in session' in the school of adversity, our place as one among many in the body of Christ will allow others to bring encouragement and support. No doubt we've already offered the same to them. It's sad, therefore, that, if asked to list the past month's afflictions, there are church leaders and members who might wish to mention one or two relating to the behaviour of other Christians. Brothers and sisters in Christ, this is not how it's meant to be! Hurting people hurt people, so, if we're welcoming hurting people into God's family (and I hope we are), there will be times when we and others are hurt. However, as part of cooperating with God's renovation process and seeking to learn all we can in this 'school', we may find it fruitful to ask him whether, for example, our own 'me first' attitudes or our low irritation thresholds and readiness to take offence are adding to our difficulties—and maybe also creating distressing 'learning opportunities' for others.

If, let's say, we sense that resentment is mounting regarding someone's attitude or behaviour, whether within the church or in another setting, we could ask specifically for insight. I am indebted to the late Father Thomas Green SJ for his wise words on many issues, and particularly for suggesting this prayer: 'Lord, let me be just as disturbed about this situation (or this person's behaviour) as you are, no more and no less. If you are angry, let me be angry too. But if you are not disturbed, let me share your peace.' He continues, 'It is amazing, and quite humbling, how often my disturbance simply dissolves once I say that prayer and really mean it' (Thomas H. Green, *Darkness in the Marketplace*, p. 103).

By passing on this prayer, I'm not pursing the line that, if we really trust God, we'll be transported to a mystical world in which everyone sees everyone else's point of view, trouble doesn't exist, and pain doesn't really hurt. Far from it! The main purpose of this chapter is to highlight how God is able to turn very real adversities around to serve his purposes, if we let him. They include the minor aggravations of life and what Green evocatively calls 'the sandpaper of failure and frustration' (p. 102), as well as the hammer-blow tragedies. We may eventually come to see that God has been using the very difficulties we've been wanting him (or lawyers!) to bring to an end, to ready us for future challenges for which we would otherwise have been ill-prepared.

Endurance and perseverance

We may prefer to believe otherwise, but the capacity to endure is developed not by an untroubled existence but by learning to press on through difficulties. God incarnate in Jesus experienced ordinary adversities, presumably including the death of his earthly father-figure, Joseph, before beginning the public ministry that led to the cross. As was said of old, 'Gold is tried in the fire, and acceptable men in the furnace of adversity' (Ecclesiasticus 2:5, KJV). Of Jesus it was written, 'Though he was God's Son, he learned trusting-obedience by what he suffered, just as we do' (Hebrews 5:8, THE MESSAGE). No one ever said life was going to be easy.

Primarily, it's our response to life's challenges, rather than the challenges themselves, that determines whether or not we grow stronger through them. When Peter writes about perseverance (2 Peter 1:6; Greek: *hypomone*, sometimes translated 'patience' or 'endurance'), he is not advocating a glum passivity—sitting it out with gritted teeth. The nature of Christian perseverance is active: cooperating with God while looking forward in trust, drawing energy from hope rooted in the faithfulness of the God of hope. Speaking of the good soil ('those with a noble and good heart') in the parable of the sower, Jesus linked perseverance with fruitfulness (Luke 8:15). God-directed perseverance (as opposed to stoicism or common-or-garden stubbornness) can be relied upon to pay off—although not necessarily in the way we may have been anticipating.

Today, the easy option often finds favour: fair enough, for those who are free agents. But there are other ways of looking at things. Here, for example, Paul views it all through the lens of character development:

We continue to shout our praise even when we're hemmed in with troubles, because we know how troubles can develop passionate patience [hypomone] in us, and how that patience in turn forges the tempered steel of virtue, keeping us alert for whatever God will do next. In alert expectancy such as this, we're never left feeling shortchanged. Quite the contrary—we can't round up enough containers to hold everything God generously pours into our lives through the Holy Spirit!

ROMANS 5:3–5 (*The Message*, MY EMPHASIS)

Peter encouraged his contemporaries with a glimpse of the bigger picture: 'For a little while you may have to experience grief in various trials. Even gold is tested for genuineness by fire. The purpose of these trials is so that your trust's genuineness, which is far more valuable than perishable gold, will be judged worthy of praise, glory and honour at the revealing of Yeshua the Messiah' (1 Peter 1:6–7, CJB). He also highlighted the contribution their difficulties were making to their spiritual formation: 'Since Jesus went through everything you're going through and more, learn to think like him. Think of your sufferings as a weaning from that old sinful habit of always expecting to get your own way. Then you'll be able to live out your days free to pursue what God wants instead of being tyrannised by what you want' (4:1–2, *THE MESSAGE*).

In the same vein, James makes a plea for Jesus' apprentices to resist the temptation to look for a hassle-free life: 'You know that the testing of your faith [trust, CJB] develops perseverance. Perseverance must finish its work so that you may be mature and complete, not lacking anything' (James 1:3–4). But… but… but… On a good day, we know that we who have chosen to follow Christ serve more than just our own comfort. At other times, maybe you detect—as do I—a part within you that rails against all this enduring and persevering. If so, why not take time now to hear what Father God has to say about it? You could also assess your level of enthusiasm for being set free from the tyranny of your wants.

Let's return to Paul. Describing a particularly difficult time spent in Asia, he said, 'We felt like we'd been sent to death row, that it was all over for us. As it turned out, it was the best thing that could have happened. Instead of trusting in our own strength or wits to get out of it, we were forced to trust God totally—not a bad idea since he's the God who raises the dead!' (2 Corinthians 1:8–9, *THE MESSAGE*).

Waiting for God

Donald Winnicott, who worked with disturbed children in the mid-20th century, noted the importance for a child of coming gradually to the realisation that his or her mother had other concerns; that she was not an exclusively devoted 'perfect mother' giving no thought to anything or anyone else. As part of developing capacities important for later life, children must learn to wait. A 'good enough mother' provides loving, age-appropriate care but also allows her child gradually to experience greater delay in her response to cries or needs. Her being unable to be in two places at once usually guarantees a certain amount of waiting for the child!

It's interesting to relate Winnicott's work to our relationship with Father God. He is all-powerful and omnipresent, yet he still allows his children the experience of waiting for him to act. Within a relationship of trust, we may assume that this is, at least in part, because he knows the beneficial effect on our capacities. If this idea is new to you, you could pause to mull it over before continuing. Often, the waiting is more easily understood with hindsight, but some delays we may never understand this side of heaven.

In his book *Life from Death Emerging*, Paul Bradbury shares personal and theological reflections set in train by the birth of his first son. Jacob failed to thrive and was prone to infection but the correct diagnosis was slow in coming. He became increasingly unwell to the point where, in a hospital room, 'life remained suspended and death hung in the air' (p. 52). Bradbury describes the frightening vulnerability brought about by not knowing where they were heading as a family, their inability to plan for the future and the painful questions about God that surfaced.

We did not believe that Jacob was now in the hands of fate but very much in the hand of God the Father… We believed that within this state of delay, in which we were powerless, we could call on an all-knowing, all-powerful God whose nature and heart led him to heal and restore. God would surely be the means by which our delay would swiftly end and normality be restored… Yet our experience was far from this apparently defendable claim… Why were so many prayers apparently unanswered and the delay allowed to go on? Were we expected to pray? Did it make any difference? (pp. 64–65)

The journey that Paul and his wife Emily travelled within the confines of that hospital ward led not only to previously unplumbed depths but also to a sense of how their experience connected with that of others and with scripture. Having reflected on John 11, and Martha and Mary's 'if only you had come more quickly' reaction to Jesus after the death of Lazarus, Bradbury comments:

This is the experience of delay—doubt, confusion, disappointment, anger, for some even a loss of faith. In delay the disjunction between the God we thought we knew and the God of our experience proves too much. Yet delay can also be a time of great growth and refinement, although often we only sense this in retrospect… I can sense now with my present perspective that that experience of waiting will remain one of the most enriching times of my life in terms of my understanding of God and my faith in him. (p. 66)

Bradbury describes delay as 'a revelatory process' and 'one of God's ways of lovingly ensuring that we discover more about him' (p. 74). He has concluded that we are richer for such times (p. 75)—and that has been my experience also. (We have already seen that this is a recurring theme in scripture.) Mother Basilea, founder of the Sisterhood in Darmstadt, Germany, frequently testified that 'with God, suffering is never the final outcome'. As the apostle Paul wrote, 'This is why we do not lose courage. Though our outer self is heading for decay, our inner self is being renewed daily. For our light and transient troubles are achieving for us an everlasting glory whose weight is beyond description. We concentrate not on what is seen but on what is not seen, since things seen are temporary, but things not seen are eternal' (2 Corinthians 4:16–17, CJB).

Settled hearts and minds

The mindset we adopt while waiting for God may be a factor in determining the course of events. Think of Job: if, amid the devastation of his home and family, he'd adopted his wife's view that he might as well 'curse God and die' (Job 2:9), the outcome could have been very different. When we need to remain steadfast, a godly mindset is useful—rather like an invisible splint. For example, when David says in Psalm 16:8, 'I have set the Lord always before me. Because he is at my right hand, I shall not be shaken', he is demonstrating a mindset found in many of the psalms, which may be summarised, 'However it looks, God is faithful and is to be trusted.' Now, David does moan from time to time, and he does sometimes ask when God is going to turn up and sort things out, but he is working from the 'given' that God is faithful. He doesn't keep weighing up whether or not to trust God.

An unexplained deterioration in my health began in 2005. In twelve months I lost ten kilos in weight without trying. No clear diagnosis was forthcoming. Everything felt like an uphill struggle. Writing another book was out of the question and

I stopped accepting speaking engagements. What did the future hold? My experience at that time, of God being close enough to lean upon, and my need for him to be so, is echoed in Bradbury's description of God as 'necessarily tangible and present' (*Life from Death Emerging*, p. 75). During the three years of waiting for the cause of my illness (an enzyme deficiency) to be revealed, I found that rehearsing in my heart the truth that God is faithful and is to be trusted promoted peace and soul-rest. Now, as I move towards better health, this habit remains a blessing. When something unexpected comes out of the blue, I can be jolted into less constructive self-talk but, encouragingly, it now takes less time to find my way back from it.

It's interesting to note how many of the things Jesus said to his disciples were aimed at developing settled hearts and minds so that, in the heat of a crisis, they wouldn't have to weigh up whether or not to trust God. A good example is when Jesus said to them, 'When you are brought before synagogues, rulers and authorities, do not worry about how you will defend yourselves or what you will say, for the Holy Spirit will teach you at that time what you should say' (Luke 12:11–12; see also 21:12–19). We see this teaching bearing fruit when Peter and the others were brought before the Sanhedrin. They had 'set minds'—set on God, his truth and his ways. Despite being flogged and ordered not to speak in the name of Jesus, they didn't spend time deliberating. They simply said, 'We must obey God rather than men' (Acts 5:29).

This aspect of Jesus' teaching also emphasises the wisdom of renouncing self-protection, as mentioned in the previous chapter. If the Lord has been speaking to you about this, you could ask him to highlight relevant verses as you read the Gospels, and to use them to settle your heart into a habitual position of trust. (Writing them in a journal could help you to keep them in mind.) You could also pray that when the unexpected happens, your immediate thought may be something along the lines of, 'OK, Lord, what do you have in mind here?'

Another theme from Jesus' teaching, relevant to this context, is what he said about temptation. His advice to his disciples was, 'Stay alert; be in prayer so you don't wander into temptation without even knowing you're in danger' (Matthew 26:41, THE MESSAGE). Temptation, even if resisted, can be unsettling. No doubt that's why Jesus made mention of it in the prayer he taught his disciples (Matthew 6:13). Paul, too, advised fleeing various sorts of temptation (1 Corinthians 6:18; 10:14; 1 Timothy 6:9–11; 2 Timothy 2:22–23). A settled mind, which knows that God will not let me be tempted beyond what I can bear and trusts him to provide a way out (1 Corinthians 10:13), is less likely to succumb to 'evil desire' (James 1:13–15).

Bread for the journey

In an acute emergency, we may expect our faithful God to provide strength and carry us through, even if we're finding it difficult to sense his presence. When thoughts and feelings are all over the place or numbed by shock, it's such a blessing to have, already formed deep in our inner being, an assurance that God is to be trusted. And, in times of turmoil, the company of those whose lives and attitudes speak of God's love can heighten our awareness of him and of his care for us. (See my book *Building the Body*, BRF, 2002, for more on how we may encourage one another as fellow members of Christ's body.)

It's also a blessing to be alert to evidence of God's hand in our surroundings, seeing beyond to the God who chose to create a world in which gratuitous beauty is everywhere—even at a microscopic level and in the depths of the earth and the ocean where no human eye will ever see. God-given beauty, whether on a small scale in the intense colour of a patch of violets or generously painted across a sunset sky, ministers refreshment to my soul. I've learned to 'bless all that is good', taking the opportunity to thank God for good and beautiful things and wise or helpful actions, whenever I notice them. A stranger who holds open the door for me and my baggage is worth thanking God for, and noticing that blessing will interrupt any grumbling inner dialogue (about travel delays or other pressures of the moment), prompting a more edifying focus.

This isn't 'the power of positive thinking'. It's about choosing, amid the pressures of life, to go on celebrating the blessedness of being 'careless in the care of God' (Matthew 6:26, THE MESSAGE), of being held and provided for by an all-powerful, trustworthy, loving Father. When it comes to evidence of his care, it's up to us to cultivate the habit of noticing the many and varied ways in which he provides for us. Father God doesn't want us just to get by on a starvation diet. He knows our needs: he has even anticipated them.

If you wished, you could reflect on what you've read so

far in this chapter while making bread—maybe sharing the experience with a friend or a small group. This exercise works to some extent using your imagination but, if you've never made bread, why not welcome along someone to share their expertise? Notice the bringing together of carefully chosen and weighed ingredients to make a loaf of a particular type. Be aware of the importance of the period of kneading: do you know what is happening to the dough at this point? Then there's the waiting—first, for the dough to rise. In our hurry-sick world, this feels so *slow*! Eventually, there's the smell of freshly baked bread, which seems to have almost universal appeal.

During the bread-making process, there will be plenty of time to listen to God and to ask what he wants to show you through it. Depending on the size and nature of your group, you could agree to keep silence for one or two periods. Here are a few questions worth considering. God created your inmost being and his eye has been upon you since before you were born (Psalm 139:13–16), but have you also felt at times as if you were being 'kneaded' by him along the way? How have you coped with the waiting times, especially when not much seemed to be happening? Have you been aware of receiving 'bread for the journey' from God? Is the reality of Jesus as 'the bread of life' part of your experience? (Reflecting on John 6 in this context could be very helpful; the same applies to Isaiah 55.) As those who are in the process of having Christ formed in them, what might it be like for your group to be 'the aroma of Christ' (2 Corinthians 2:14–15) to the people around? Finally, how may the finished bread (and perhaps also the story of its making) be shared to bring blessing?

Praying during times of testing

In times of adversity, prayer may become impossible on account of physical or mental fragility, lack of concentration or exhaustion. The rhythm of prayer that usually sustains us may be disrupted. Brothers and sisters in Christ can support us in prayer but it's also true that, at such times, when we're unable to put the cries of our hearts into words, God still hears them. Please read what follows in the light of that truth, and not as implying that unless we 'pray proper prayers' God won't hear us.

In recent years I've learned the value of single-line prayers. Pastor John Mulinde from Uganda, who brought blessing during my illness by expanding my understanding of covenant and of God's enduring faithfulness, taught us to pray, 'Jesus, my mighty covenant partner, fight for me!' I can't recall how I learned to pray, 'Jesus, anchor me!' but in three words it sums up the choice to trust God in circumstances that feel overwhelming.

Praying scripture can be a blessing, especially in times of disorientation. Paul's letters record prayers prayed for those to whom he was writing. These and many others (including in the Psalms) may help when we're struggling to find words. Even those who in normal circumstances see written prayers as a straitjacket may value them in testing times. A line or two from the Lord's Prayer, such as 'Your kingdom come, your will be done', may be all we can manage, but, when we've no idea what is going on or where we are heading, lining up our will with God's is powerful. It shows where we're choosing to stand.

Finally, I've already suggested prayers along the lines of 'Father, please expand my heart's capacity to…'. I've found it constructive to pray in this way, especially when hearing myself say something like, 'I wish I were more…' (whatever it happens to be at that time). Turning the thought into a prayer acknowledges what can, in the goodness and grace of God, become a reality—which is much more worthwhile than simply sighing about it. Is there something you'd like to express to God now—something he's been putting on your heart—using a one-line prayer? 'Father, please expand my heart's capacity to_____.'

THE FRUIT OF THE SPIRIT

Now for two more aspects of Jesus' character: patience and kindness.

In Ancient Greece, patience was not regarded as a virtue. What about today? We may speak of 'hanging on in there' when adversity is taking its toll, but too often patience is equated with passive resignation or seen as a weakness to be exploited. Those who admit to lacking patience often mean that they hate queuing or that they exhibit a childish inability to delay gratification ('I want it *now*!'). Although the old rhyme still tells us that 'patience is a virtue', there's little awareness of what genuine patience looks like in practice.

The New Testament word translated patience, *makrothumia*, and others related to it, lack exact English equivalents, but scriptural references to them can contribute to our understanding. In the Greek version of the Old Testament, God is repeatedly described as *makrothumos*, often translated 'slow to anger'. For example, 'The Lord is compassionate and gracious, slow to anger, abounding in love' (Psalm 103:8). This reflects the literal meaning of the word, which is 'long temper'. The New Testament also bears witness to God's patience: Peter writes, 'The Lord... is patient with you, not wanting anyone to perish, but everyone to come to repentance' (2 Peter 3:9). The writer to the Hebrews urges his readers to 'imitate those who through faith and patience inherit what has been promised' (Hebrews 6:12). Here, the Amplified Bible is particularly glorious, counselling believers to follow the example of 'those who through faith [that is, by their leaning of the entire personality on God in Christ in absolute trust and confidence in His power, wisdom and goodness], and by practice of patient endurance *and* waiting are [now] inheriting the promises'.

We are to bear patiently not only with events but also with people. Think of Jesus' attitude to his disciples. Peter put his foot in it on several occasions that we know about and probably many more of which we know nothing; Thomas was pessimistic and then couldn't recognise good news when he heard it (John 11:16; 20:25). Jesus was not blind to their failings, yet he stuck with them—and with others, including Judas. God shows the same enduring patience with each one of us, you and me included.

This has implications for our life together in God's family. We may not realise it but, when we accept Christ as our Saviour, we enter into an indissoluble relationship with all other Christians. It seems appropriate to borrow a line from the marriage service: from that day forward, 'for better, for worse; for richer, for poorer; in sickness and in health', we are brothers and sisters in Christ and members of Christ's body, the Church (1 Corinthians 12:12–13). In a passage that makes mention of the effort necessary to keep our unity in good repair, Paul reminds 'the saints in Ephesus' to 'be patient, bearing with one another in love' (Ephesians 1:1; 4:2–6). Yes, patience and other Spirit-given qualities are indispensable within the community of God's people. If, at the moment, conflict within your local church is giving cause for concern, why not use these verses as a springboard into prayer?

William Barclay writes evocatively of the qualities that *makrothumia* represents. He links them with the great-heartedness of magnanimity, adding that some translators have tried to invent the word 'longanimity'. In a comment that has relevance also to the first part of this chapter, Barclay observes that 'the hardest lesson of all' may be 'to learn... how to wait when nothing seems to be happening, and when all the circumstances seem calculated to bring nothing but discouragement' (*Flesh and Spirit*, p. 91). Barclay goes on to say:

The Christian must be like the prophets who again and again had to wait for the action of God; he must be like the farmer who sows the seed and who then through the slow months waits until the harvest comes (James 5:7–10). It may be that this is the hardest task of all for an age which has made a god of speed.
FLESH AND SPIRIT, P. 96

Lest patience be associated only with prolonged waiting in difficult circumstances, imagine a father hovering behind a child who is learning to ride a bicycle. He's prepared either to grab hold if wobbles become too severe or to whoop with delight at signs of progress. Is that father conscious of being patient or long-suffering? Probably not! So, as we take note of how the Holy Spirit once again seeks to form in us a characteristic of God himself, let's recall the Father's delight—not just his forbearance—and allow ourselves to be surprised afresh by joy.

Kindness (*chrestotes*) is also a characteristic of God (see, for example, Romans 2:4; Ephesians 2:7; Titus 3:4). It's one of the list of attributes with which Paul tells us, as God's chosen people, to clothe ourselves (Colossians 3:12; for an explanation of 'clothe', see the third Bible reflection at the end of this chapter). Elsewhere, in a passage in which Paul uses several Old Testament quotations to express his dismay, he specifically mentions the lack of *chrestotes* (in this case, referred to as 'doing good'): 'All have turned away, they have together become worthless; there is no one who does good, not even one' (Romans 3:12; quoting Psalm 14:3). Bear in mind that what is being referred to in this section is a kindly *disposition*, a heart-appetite for all that is good. The focus is not on doing lots of good, kind actions, although kindness may well be manifested in such ways.

In the Middle Ages, the Church taught about the seven contrary virtues, the antitheses of the seven deadly sins. Kindness (Latin: *humanitas*) was seen as contrary in spirit to envy (an ill-will which, at its most venomous, seeks the destruction of the good that is being envied). *Humanitas* is humankind at its best—not as in the sentiment 'We're all nice really; I'm sure God will let everyone into heaven', but in the sense that, in showing kindness, men and women offer a glimpse of what it means to be made in the image of God. Even a remnant of the image can offer an occasional pinpoint of light. As we who, in Christ, have been created anew (2 Corinthians 5:17) allow Father, Son and Holy Spirit to make their home with us, their influence will bear fruit in our lives and we will increasingly be able to show God-honouring and God-revealing *humanitas*.

'Be kind to each other, tender-hearted; and forgive each other,' says Paul, 'just as in the Messiah God has also forgiven you' (Ephesians 4:32, CJB). Our kindness is not only inspired by but both encircled and eclipsed by the heart of our kind and forgiving God. It could be helpful to memorise this verse (or your preferred version of it) and carry it in your mind as you go about your daily activities. Don't come under condemnation when you become aware of falling short. Rather, pray, 'Jesus, friend of sinners, forgive me for _____, and grow and nourish your kindness in me.'

BIBLE REFLECTIONS

1. Read Isaiah 37:9–20.

Hezekiah's response was to take his adversary's threatening letter to God without delay, to look 'up and out' of his diffi-culties. Keep this picture in mind during the day as events unfold. Is there a dilemma, a difficulty or a delight that you'd like to 'spread before the Lord' as Hezekiah did?

2. Read 1 Corinthians 9:24–27 in *THE MESSAGE* (as below). Read slowly, visualising the images depicted:

You've all been to the stadium and seen the athletes race. Everyone runs; one wins. Run to win. All good athletes train hard. They do it for a gold medal that tarnishes and fades. You're after one that's gold eternally. I don't know about you, but I'm running hard for the finishing line. I'm giving it everything I've got. No sloppy living for me! I'm staying alert and in top condition. I'm not going to get caught napping, telling everyone else all about it and then missing out myself.

Now pick out words and phrases that illustrate 'running to win', 'sloppy living' and their divergent consequences. We'll be looking more closely at the place of effort and discipline in following Jesus in Chapter 5. Does God want to say anything to you in preparation? Rereading this passage now and then would be a way of showing him that you're open to hearing. If you're struggling with ideas found in the passage, you could express your feelings to God, then listen to what he has to say.

3. Read Colossians 3:12–17.
Note that when Paul says, 'clothe yourselves with' and 'put on', there's no sense of dressing up in order to conceal undesirable characteristics. The Greek verb is *enduo* and the sense is of being active participants, clothing ourselves with God's provision. Paul uses the same word to tell us to put on 'the armour of light' (Romans 13:12), 'the full armour of God' (Ephesians 6:11), 'faith and love as a breastplate, and

the hope of salvation as a helmet' (1 Thessalonians 5:8).

Make a list of the characteristics of God's people from this passage, then take time to be still before him. Thank him for his patience and kindness, and ask him which of these 'articles of clothing' he wants to provide for you right now. Focus on what he has for you, not on how grubby or inadequate you feel. If you can't get past your own inadequacies, talk to God about them, but make sure you also listen to what he says in reply. When you're ready, tell Father God that you're ready to receive, and thank him for his provision.

4

TRANSFORMED THROUGH WORSHIP AND PRAYER

If you struggle with worshipping or praying, or with both, please don't assume that this chapter isn't for you. While many of Jesus' followers have difficulty with certain styles and practices, I'm aware that others perennially feel the odd one out, unable to engage much or at all—and the fact that everyone else seems to be doing fine just makes it worse. As children of God, we all have the capacity to worship and pray—yes, all of us—but capacities need developing if they're to be fruitful. Some sincere followers of Jesus try hard, very hard. They've read books (mostly written by non-strugglers) and tried following the schemes suggested, but they still feel they've failed.

Prayer and worship are foundational to being and expressing who we are as God's children. What's more, our participation contributes to the shaping of the people we're becoming. You may have noticed that I'm into my second paragraph without mentioning saying prayers or singing songs. I will be referring to them, of course—they have an important place in the lives of Jesus' apprentices—but it's vital to understand that the worship and prayer that contribute to our shaping are more than just activities to be engaged in for a period and then ticked off as 'done' until the next appointed time. I find it helpful to see them as continuous threads running through everyday life, threads that glorify God and further his kingdom purposes, serving both to anchor and to orientate us.

The following illustration may help. If you've ever fiddled with a portable television aerial, you'll know the importance of orientation in making the link with the transmitter. This determines whether the picture comes through without distortion or, indeed, at all. It's like that with our hearts: their orientation really matters, and not just at times marked out for prayer or worship. If our hearts are orientated towards God, we'll find ourselves engaging in worship and prayer in diverse settings. (The Bible records examples taking place in the innards of a whale, a prison cell and the middle of nowhere, as well as in more traditional locations.) Orientation also triumphs over distance: if we've wandered off, once we choose—despite potential distractions, fears or other turbulent emotions—to turn and set our faces in the right direction, we'll find Father God coming out to meet us.

In passing, let's note just how much Jesus' attitude to prayer and worship surprised his contemporaries. He met with his Father both in the imposing setting of the temple and out in the countryside. When a Samaritan woman began to quiz Jesus about whether worship should be carried out in one particular place or another, he responded (shockingly countercultural on several fronts!) by telling her that the time had come for 'true worshippers' to 'worship the Father in spirit and truth, for they are the kind of worshippers the Father seeks' (John 4:23). It could be salutary to reflect on how complicated the Church has been making things ever since, and how often arguments about externals have hijacked the focus.

Jesus saw greater value in a widow's minuscule worship offering than in the grand donations of the rich (Luke 21:1–4), and told a story about how the one-line prayer of a tax collector begging for mercy was heard by God (18:9–14; tax collectors were despised for collaborating with the occupying Roman power). Jesus appalled the chief priests and the teachers of the law by accepting what amounted to worship from noisy children (Matthew 21:15–16). He met with fellow Jews in the temple and at the synagogue, where he was allowed to read the scriptures and to teach. Yet Jesus was willing to face official disapproval for breaking the rules by healing a man's hand and releasing a woman from being bent double on the sabbath (Luke 6:6–11; 13:10–17).

In a book of this kind, it's not possible to cover all that Jesus said and did in relation to worship and prayer. If you know that these are areas of difficulty for you, researching Jesus' attitudes and actions for yourself is likely to bring both clarification and blessing. You could, for example, read Luke's Gospel and make a note of everything Jesus did or said relating to worship or prayer, and use those notes as the starting point for a conversation with God.

'The Lord is here'

Anglican liturgy affirms the presence of God by his Spirit when the church gathers. 'The Lord is here,' says the service leader, and the members of the congregation respond, 'His

Spirit is with us', irrespective of the views they hold on the role of the Holy Spirit. Yet some Christians struggle to sense God's presence in church, let alone in non-church settings. Women and men who were physically or emotionally abandoned or abused as children, and those who, as adults, have been traumatised by divorce or bereavement, often find it difficult to know for sure that God is with them. They, and the many others who struggle in this way, may find it a relief to hear that although God's children are urged to seek him out, this kind of seeking is nothing like pursuing a reluctant parent who has no wish to spend time with them.

God is not absent: it's primarily a matter of our awareness. King David marvelled at finding God at every turn, asking, 'Where can I go from your Spirit? Where can I flee from your presence? If I go up to the heavens, you are there; if I make my bed in the depths, you are there. If I rise on the wings of the dawn, if I settle on the far side of the sea, even there your hand will guide me, your right hand will hold me fast' (Psalm 139:7–10). The coming Messiah was spoken of by the prophet Isaiah using the name Immanuel, which means 'God with us' (Isaiah 7:14; Matthew 1:23). As we welcome him in faith, thoughts and feelings eventually catch up; it becomes easier to sense God's presence once we've started taking it on trust that he is with us. So, how many ways can you think of in which to welcome God's presence, right here, right now?

When God seems unresponsive or distant, and our prayers go apparently unanswered, is this a valid reason for changing our view of him or withholding worship? Worship that is results-based rather than a response to God himself has unstable footings. Job had grasped this fact (Job 1:20–22) but many around him during his trials had not. We may also learn from Daniel and his friends, who demonstrated, in extreme circumstances, that their worship was not conditional on God turning up to save them (see Daniel 3 and 6). Our worship is due to almighty God because of who he is—'the great unchangeable I AM', as one hymn writer has put it ('Before the throne of God above', Charitie Lees Bancroft, 1863). Why not spend a few minutes now, calling to mind phrases used in scripture (or scripture-based hymns and songs) to describe God, celebrating his goodness and greatness and his abiding presence? You could start with 'Bless the Lord, O my soul!' (Psalm 103:1, KJV).

In circumstances that we do not understand, continuing worship reinforces a heart-attitude of trust. Remember, we're only really trusting God when we have no idea what he's up to; if we know what he's doing, we're merely agreeing to go along with his plan. If we're unwilling to worship while waiting, we're vulnerable to distraction by a sneaky voice suggesting that God might be withholding good from us to our detriment, which may send us off in a very different direction.

Losing the plot—and being found

Church leader, preacher and author A.W. Tozer was, above all else, a worshipper. In a recent book, compiled from audio recordings discovered long after his death, he gives a sense of the communion that Adam and Eve enjoyed with God in those first heady days:

They had an exclusive on God shared by no other part of God's creation. Unlike everything else in this mystic and marvellous world of God's creation, Adam and Eve could worship God and God anticipated that worship. In the cool of the day, God came down and walked with Adam and Eve in the garden of Eden where they joyously offered their reverence and adoration.
THE WORSHIP-DRIVEN LIFE, P. 22

Tozer contrasts this joyful existence with what came afterwards, bringing 'a terrific sense of disorientation, resulting in spiritual amnesia' (p. 23).

The loss of intimate fellowship with God started when Adam and Eve listened to another voice (Genesis 3:1), a voice suggesting that God might be depriving them of something good. Rebellion swiftly followed; they were refocused, with disastrous consequences. Tozer notes the parallels to this 'spiritual amnesia' in the experience of a man waking from a coma brought about by a mugging (p. 25). With no evidence of identity and a blanked-out memory, he has no perspective on life and no purpose. He has no idea what he was doing in the place where he was mugged; he doesn't even know his own name. The robbery is complete.

The rest of the Bible chronicles God's response, his rescue plan. Within this plan, prayer and worship are foundational in the sense that they serve to remind us 'which way is up'—that God is in charge; that he is good and worthy of our praise. Prayer and worship are also foundational in that they emphasise *whose* we are, and that we are no longer lost but found. By anchoring us in our true identity, they open up the way not only to intimacy with God but also to a purposeful future. God-focused worship and prayer, permeating our lives, will determine the kind of people we become as we walk forward into that future.

So, where do we start? We come from different places, from different cultural backgrounds and traditions, with different mindsets, yet we may all begin by affirming that we are God's much-loved children, saved by his grace and with an open invitation to approach him. If we feel like hiding from God, as Adam and Eve did after their great debacle, it would be good to ask him if there is any sin we've overlooked, which is causing us to want to distance ourselves. We may take it for granted that, whatever the problem, the answer is not to try to hide it or ourselves from God.

A life of worship

Professor David Augsburger of Fuller Theological Seminary notes that, in the Anabaptist tradition (among others), the communal spirituality of disciples is 'lived out in a distinctive cluster of traits or practices expressed in daily life, in work and in play—all experienced as worship. These seven are radical attachment, stubborn loyalty, tenacious serenity, habitual humility, resolute non-violence, concrete service, and authentic witness.' He comments, 'It is a spirituality of the feet, the knees, the hands, and the spine as well as the heart and the head... a form of visible, not invisible spirituality, of action as embodied love and truth, worked out in everyday life "with a proper sense of awe and responsibility"' (Philippians 2:12, JBP; *Dissident Discipleship: A Spirituality of Self-Surrender, Love of God, and Love of Neighbour*, pp. 20–21). This kind of worship will shape the worshippers.

J.B. Phillips' translation of Philippians 2:12, quoted by Augsburger, is instructive in its inclusion of the word '*awe*', about which I shall say more shortly. You may be more familiar with a translation that says something like 'Continue to work out your salvation with fear and trembling' (NIV). But had you made the connection between this day-by-day 'working out' and living a life of worship? Pause for a moment and consider the opportunities that will be presenting themselves in what remains of today for, say, 'serenity as worship'. How might this link up with what the Lord was saying to you as you reflected on learning to trust him and being formed through adversity?

I find it encouraging to remember that the worship in heaven never ceases. So when I lift my heart in worship to God in the middle of whatever I'm doing or when unable to sleep in the early hours, I'm joining with the chorus of the heavenly host. I have no need to 'begin' anything or, indeed, to bring anything to a close; when I'm worshipping, I'm part of something greater—so much greater! It's like the instruments in a very large orchestra, each contributing to the melody or the harmonies at various points, and at all times, silent or not, being part of the group. However, this picture falls down because there will be no packing up and dispersing: we'll be continuing to worship God for eternity.

Awe and devotion

Regardless of how others use the word today, I refuse to describe anyone other than God as 'awesome'. Dictionary definitions of the word 'awe' include comments about the power to control those who are awed—highly relevant to our consideration of the transforming power of worship.

At school, children take on the habits, mannerisms and speech patterns of older pupils whom they want to be like one day. From time to time, concern is expressed about the unruly or unpleasant behaviour of sporting heroes, because of the effect it may be having on their young fans. Celebrities with unhealthy lifestyles come in for criticism for similar reasons. Parents of a teenage girl who is slavishly modelling herself upon a pop or fashion icon may be heard lamenting her fixation on her 'idol', but are they aware that their daughter is enacting the age-old spiritual principle of becoming like whatever it is we worship? When we worship someone (even if we don't call it 'worship'), we give them power to direct our thinking, our behaviour and our being. The person may be one whose purposes are laudable and life-affirming, such as a Bible teacher. Yet it's still true that holding them in awe, which should be reserved for God alone, puts the relationship on an unhealthy footing.

Thinking back to William Barclay's comment (see p. 87) that our age has 'made a god of speed', how might putting 'speed' in charge affect a person, their family, their work environment and colleagues, or their community? The same might also be asked about possessions. It's said that we do not possess things we are unable to give away: they possess us. (Luke 12:15 is relevant here.) The question I posed in the Introduction is pertinent: 'Who or what is shaping the way I think, feel and live?' We need to be willing for God and our nearest and dearest to speak truth to us if our devotion to a person, a cause, an activity or a possession (or to possessions in general) is distancing us from them.

My book *Driven Beyond the Call of God* (BRF, 1999) deals more fully with the spiritual issues involved in allowing anything or anyone other than God to be in charge of our lives, but it's appropriate to mention them briefly here. We may find it difficult to relate to the practices of those who made idols out of wood or metal and then worshipped them (see Psalm 135:15–18), but look around: devoted attachment to inanimate objects is not only part of our culture but is also heavily promoted by the media. Ask yourself: what am I currently being assured I cannot live without? Bring into consciousness the emotions stirred by the thought of giving up TV, the internet or your favourite sport or hobby for even a month. Where do you turn for comfort if you're having a seriously bad week? Is it to a particular friend who always 'fixes it' for you, or to chocolate, alcohol, computer gaming, a workout at the gym, or something else? If this is a regular pattern, it will be having a deforming influence on you and on those who are influenced by your example.

Finally on this topic, as outlined above, we tend to take on the characteristics of those we regard with awe, so the way we perceive the God we worship really does matter. If we're becoming like the authentic Jesus, who is described as full of grace and truth (John 1:14), then all is well. But if, as we worship, we are, for example, seeking to distance ourselves from Christians from other social or ethnic backgrounds or filling up with hatred towards those who see things differently, then we must examine whether the object of our worship is the God of love whom Jesus revealed.

God-focused prayer

Let's turn now to the subject of prayer. Rueben Job notes the diverse approaches to prayer among the people known to him, yet he also sees 'a unifying constant... a movement toward God that results in transformation of life and how life is valued and lived out in the everyday experiences of our existence' (*Three Simple Rules*, p. 66).

It's clear from Paul's letter to the Christians at Philippi that he recognised the formative effect of prayer (Philippians 4:6–7). Paul advised keeping hearts and minds orientated towards God, bringing any difficulties to him rather than allowing them to hijack the focus. I've found the picture of shaping worries into prayers (in THE MESSAGE; see page 68 of this book) to be very fruitful. It really is true that if you know how to worry, you're well on the way to praying—that is, if you're willing to direct concerns towards God instead of rehearsing them in a destructive, circular, inner monologue.

Father God has said, 'Ask', so there's no doubt that we're free to ask and to go on asking, but I've learned that it can also be right to leave a particular concern with God. Leanne Payne, in her writing and teaching on healing prayer, stresses the importance of looking 'up and out' of our difficulties rather than allowing them to take centre stage in our thinking. So yes, times of prayer may include bringing our difficulties to God repeatedly and persistently, but let's ask the Lord to alert us if 'persisting in prayer' has become extended self-focused worrying expressed in religious language. Worrying causes trust to leach away, whereas God-focused praying builds trust, relationship and much more.

Over time, God-focused prayer shapes us, not least because it nourishes and strengthens the Christ-life within us. Being part of a praying community will shape us even more effectively.

Praying communities shape lives

When Jesus' disciples asked him to teach them to pray, he steered them away from the methodology of the experts towards something that began with an expression of relationship: 'Father' (Matthew 6:9). It's within our relationship with Father God that we may expect our personal transformation to take place. However, it's no accident that the prayer Jesus taught begins with 'Our' and continues using plural words ('our', 'us'): God loves to see families, friends and communities approaching him *together*. Each time two or three or more of God's people come together to pray to their one heavenly Father, community foundations are strengthened.

It's widely recognised that community events and concerted community actions communicate powerfully to children, even when they understand very little and are too young to put into words what is happening. So imagine being a youngster in a nation about to be overrun by an alliance of powerful warmongers. The situation appears hopeless. Your king's response has been to call everyone to fast. Men, women and children are assembling in the central place of worship. The king stands up and prays a short prayer, ending, 'For we have no power to face this vast army that is attacking us. We do not know what to do, but our eyes are upon you' (2 Chronicles 20:12).

Now imagine being a youngster during World War II at the time of the Allied Forces' landing in Normandy. Your family is huddled round a crackling radio, waiting for the king to speak. You don't catch it all, but you hear him say, 'What is demanded from us all is something more than courage, more than endurance: we need a revival of spirit, a new unconquerable resolve.' King George VI goes on, 'That we may be worthily matched with this new summons of destiny, I desire solemnly to call my people to prayer and dedication. We are not unmindful of our own shortcomings past and present. We shall ask not that God may do our will, but that we may be enabled to do the will of God.'

Spend a few minutes imagining how these national events might have contributed to the formation of attitudes in the young people of the day, and to the development of their beliefs about where it is normal to turn in times of trouble.

One final point on this theme: neighbours, friends and men and women in the wider community who do not acknowledge God, when faced with serious ill health, sometimes start asking the church to pray. Their request may be as a result of contact at the time of a wedding or a funeral. It may also follow an earlier occasion on which a church member, made aware of a need, had said to their friend, neighbour, car mechanic or hairdresser, 'Would you like me to pray about that?' This offer had let them know that it would be OK to ask. Some people come to trust Jesus for themselves through such prayer requests. Others continue to ask while 'standing outside'—for now, at least.

Prayer in practice

Some of us are, by personality, better at following patterns than being spontaneous (or vice versa). You probably know which you find easier. In my experience, it's helpful to think in terms of a mixture—a pattern for prayer in the midst of an ongoing dialogue with God. The proportions may differ not only among different personality types but also at different times of life. Structures and schedules come easily to me. However, in recent years when health problems have been making their presence felt, it has been the ongoing dialogue, in between the set times, that God has used to strengthen my relationship with him and bring blessing. The regular times are like the ballast keeping the ship upright—I notice if they're not there—while the ongoing dialogue is like the wind filling the sails.

I'm going to share some personal examples, but not as a template to follow. Read them as illustrations, while asking the Lord what he has in mind for you. As I mentioned in Chapter 2, I sometimes pray the Lord's Prayer if I'm awake at night. My morning begins with a few words of prayer before getting out of bed. At the time of writing, I am in the habit of saying, as I get up, 'This is the day the Lord has made; let us rejoice and be glad in it' (Psalm 118:24). My husband and I have been known to say it to one another, changing the wording to a more determined 'We *will* rejoice and be glad in it' on days that promise to be a bit of a struggle. Once out of bed, I take time to be quiet with God (reading the Bible and praying), after which I consciously walk forward with Jesus into the rest of the day.

Later on, if I find myself telling a friend about a problem I haven't already brought to God or some encouraging news for which I haven't thanked him, I make it a three-way conversation: waiting until a time set aside for prayer doesn't work. As I said in the previous chapter, my aim is to thank God whenever I'm conscious of being thankful for something or someone. I enjoy singing, so I sometimes sing songs, especially scripture-based ones, as prayers. My day ends with a couple of short readings and a brief time of reflection before God.

Pastor Ian Stackhouse writes that it's not simply a matter of scheduling prayer; rather, it's 'a rhythm of prayer... embracing the movements of God's grace as they occur to us throughout the day' (*The Day is Yours: Slow Spirituality in a Fast-Moving World*, pp. 59–60). Rueben Job tells of a friend who 'describes his life of prayer as "staying in touch with the home office"' (*Three Simple Rules*, p. 66). My friend Mary, now in her 80s and a follower of Jesus since her student days, likens prayer to 'a country walk with a friend'. If you were writing a letter to a friend about prayer, how would you describe it?

A continuum of worship and prayer

Down the centuries, God's presence amid the daily routine has been called to mind in countless different ways. Think of the Celts who, for hundreds of years, practised subsistence-level farming in inhospitable territory. They voiced prayers in a wide range of situations—milking a cow; lighting a fire and so on. 'These prayers, usually chanted or sung, were not uttered in religious contexts but rather were the songs of daily life' (J. Philip Newell, *Celtic Prayers from Iona*, p. 7). Today, many Christians take a moment to thank God at meal times. What about other opportunities for calling to mind his nearness or thanking him for his provision—for example, when switching on a light, filling the kettle with water or opening the fridge? I'm sure you can think of other examples from your own routine. (Actions connected with light, water and nourishment are particularly valuable because of their symbolic content.)

So, yes, worship and prayer are intended to be part of our response to God as life happens, but what about Sundays? Children for whom the word 'Sunday' meant a boring day with lots of 'don'ts' may have been only too pleased, as adults, to throw off what they saw as oppressive rules. When strong feelings are involved, though, there's always the danger of throwing the clean baby out with the dirty bathwater. If this could apply to you, is there a blessing waiting to be reclaimed? At its most basic, the sabbath, as God ordained it, was about pausing to remember what really mattered and to respond to him; it was time set apart to hallow all time as God's. Many have found it a blessing to return to taking sabbaths as part of a continuum of worship and prayer.

While it may be easy to worship God in times of great celebration and we may find ourselves propelled into prayer in times of crisis, when nothing much is happening inertia can so easily take over. Yet pressing on in worship and prayer when routine threatens to send us to sleep not only honours God but also attunes and trains our hearts for times when the adrenaline is pumping. If you feel you're drifting in an ocean of the mundane, how about taking the initiative, as Tozer did? As a young man, his life was enriched by worshipping God while working on an assembly line. Brother Lawrence, a 17th-century lay brother in a monastery, learned to 'practise the presence of God' during menial tasks. Moment by moment he called to mind God's presence with him, and he worshipped and prayed as he served his community. Even on his deathbed Brother Lawrence was worshipping, saying, 'I'm just doing what I've been doing for forty years and I expect to be doing throughout eternity' (*The Worship-Driven Life*, p. 48).

Brother Lawrence knew that 'the practice of the presence of God' could also be part of life in very fraught circumstances. In one of his letters, he gave advice to a woman who was concerned for a young soldier going off to war:

A small lifting of the heart suffices, a small remembrance of God, a movement of the heart's worship, though in haste and with sword in hand, are prayers, which, brief though they may be, are yet most pleasing to God, and, very far from making those engaged in battle lose their courage, in the most dangerous moments they make them brave. Let him… little by little, habituate himself to this small but holy discipline. No one sees it, and nothing is more easy than to repeat often throughout the day these small acts of worship in the heart.

THE PRACTICE OF THE PRESENCE OF GOD, PP. 48–49

What is a 'lifting of the heart'? Here is an illustration: when our elder son and his (then) fiancée were living 100 miles apart, I'm sure his heart moved in her direction quite a lot, and her heart in his. No doubt they managed to bring each other to mind in all sorts of circumstances, with no difficulty whatsoever. We may lift our hearts to God in the middle of things, too. Practising the presence of God means calling to mind the reality of God's presence with us. It's nothing particularly mystical and certainly not magical. Yes, it's a conscious effort to begin with, but once it becomes a habit it happens more frequently and easily. In practice, it feels more like a way of life—a way of being rather than a way of doing. And, as for our son and his fiancée, love rather than duty provides the impetus. I've found it a blessing to make a small lifting of my heart to God in the queue at the supermarket or while watching the TV news. You could try it when you're stuck in a traffic jam or a difficult meeting, and see the different perspective it brings.

If you've been challenged by the example of Tozer and by Brother Lawrence's encouragement to 'practise the presence of God', why not call to mind God's presence with you right now? Put to one side any self-consciousness as you do so: after all, the idea is to become more conscious of God. Don't fall into the trap of analysing what's happening. Simply engage your mind with the knowledge that God is present with you, and lift your heart to him.

The mundane may be able to send us into a mental and spiritual drift, and the heat of battle may threaten to overwhelm, but the good times may also disrupt our focus. In the case of material prosperity, it's all too easy to lose sight of God and his plans as exciting choices present themselves and are considered. Might we have a new car, a tropical holiday, a garden makeover—or maybe just put the cash in an off-shore account? (See what Jesus had to say about building bigger

barns to accommodate a bumper harvest: Luke 12:16–21.)
In such circumstances, calling to mind God's presence will
open the way for him to redirect our hearts before they
wander too far off course.

Building resilience

As illustrated by Daniel and his friends (Daniel 3 and 6),
expectant trust in a faithful God can help us to pray and
continue worshipping in challenging times, regardless of
what powerful people have said the outcome will be. The
choice to engage in worship and prayer will feed back into
greater resilience and a growing sense of being held by a
faithful God, whatever the outcome.

At a time when persecution was rife, Paul reassured his
readers that nothing would be able to separate them from
God's love (Romans 8:35–39). Reflecting on this passage,
Guy Chevreau counsels:

*The only way our hearts and hearts' affections can be so assured is
through a life of worship… As we choose to align our hearts and
hearts' affections with His we are then affirming greater faith in
God's faithfulness than faith in our present understanding of the
challenging circumstances we face.*
VITAL SIGNS OF A HEALTHY CHURCH, P. 28

Have you ever found yourself expressing greater faith in your
understanding of your circumstances than in God's faithfulness? Yes, me too! Are you ready to receive and act upon this
encouragement to live 'a life of worship' in which we 'choose

to align our hearts and hearts' affections' with God's? What might that look like in your current circumstances?

As a response to this chapter, you could pray, 'Father, please increase my capacity to align my heart with yours.'

THE FRUIT OF THE SPIRIT

As we worship the one who is love, goodness and faithfulness personified, we may expect to become more like him. If, however, we were brought up in and formed by a culture in which 'being good' had negative connotations, it's worth asking how enthusiastic we really are about embracing goodness. Wanting to avoid the label 'goody-goody' at school may have prompted us to engage in a certain amount of rebellion in the hope of blending in with our peers. As we grew older, if we lacked the chutzpah necessary for continuing rebellion, we may have settled for being nice. But 'niceness' isn't the same as 'goodness'. You could ask God to highlight any previous choices or current thought patterns that are obstructing your understanding or the work of his Spirit in you.

The Greek word *agathosune*, translated 'goodness' in Paul's list of the fruit of the Spirit, appears only four times in the New Testament. (The three other occasions are Romans 15:14; Ephesians 5:9; 2 Thessalonians 1:11.) By contrast, the corresponding adjective, *agathos*, is very common, but with a wide variety of meanings according to context—just like our English word 'good'. For example, some might call a joke 'good' even if those with 'good' taste found it silly or offensive.

After much study, William Barclay concluded that *agathosune* is 'the generosity which springs from the heart that is kind' (*Flesh and Spirit*, p. 107). Others have linked goodness with truth. The Hebrew scriptures are clear: the only one who is truly good is God. This is brought out in Jesus' response to a questioner: 'Why do you question me about what's good? *God* is the One who is good', adding, 'If you want to enter the life of God, just do what he tells you' (Matthew 19:17, THE MESSAGE). Perhaps that's a word to us, too, as we consider this aspect of the fruit of the Spirit. Let's not become so bogged down in cogitating about the meaning of goodness that we lose sight of our purpose. God is goodness personified and is looking to plant his goodness in us by his Spirit. Doing what he tells us is always good.

In Jesus' stinging critique of the spirituality of the teachers of the law and the Pharisees, he denounced them for being scrupulous in tithing herbs while neglecting 'the more important matters of the law—justice, mercy and *faithfulness*' (Matthew 23:23; my italics). Few people today will be known for tithing herbs, but I have no doubt that God is dishonoured in similar ways—for example, when more attention is paid to the choice of the choir's anthem or the onscreen backdrop for the words of the songs than to the spirit in which a community gathers for worship.

Yes, faithfulness (Greek: *pistis*; 'faith' in the KJV) includes actions, but behind the actions is so much more—a settled disposition; an attitude of the heart that predisposes us to trustworthiness in all matters, whether trivial or of national importance; a renewed mind that wastes no time weighing up the pros and cons of dubious alternatives. (Remember

Jesus' words about adultery having been committed in the heart even if no physical act has taken place: Matthew 5:28.)

God himself is faithful: the scriptures leave us in no doubt of that. As he forms his nature in us by his Spirit, we may expect our willingness to allow this to be our ruling disposition to be tested—and we will face battles to stay faithful in small things, not just in major confrontations. In an ungodly world in which many assume that those who are faithful simply lack the courage to be otherwise, we do well to spend time with and allow ourselves to be influenced by those who will bless rather than deride what God is doing in us by his Spirit.

In David Stern's version, one of David's psalms speaks of 'those who live lives of integrity', saying, 'I look to the faithful of the land, so that they can be my companions' (Psalm 101:6, CJB). Another psalm puts it like this: 'Trust in Adonai [the Lord], and do good; settle in the land, and feed on faithfulness. Then you will delight yourself in Adonai, and he will give you your heart's desire' (Psalm 37:3–4, CJB). God brought these verses to my attention some years ago as I was about to begin a sabbatical. I planned accordingly and found it restful and restorative to spend time with faithful people. By their lives and attitudes—their settled dispositions and their integrity—they supported me in my desire to stay faithful to God. Do you have sisters or brothers in Christ in whose company the same blessing comes to you? If not, you could ask God to alert you to opportunities to meet some. I have found being part of a Renovaré group tremendously valuable (see www.renovare. org for more information).

BIBLE REFLECTIONS

1. Read Matthew 5:21–24.

Here, Jesus' words about seeking reconciliation before worship relate to a specific act of worship, but they are no less relevant to ongoing prayer and heart-worship. If we choose to call to mind that God is with us and to make small liftings of our hearts towards him during the day, how will this affect our attitude to the people around us? You could take these verses into your day and mull them over at coffee and meal breaks, asking God to speak through them.

2. Read Psalm 145, aloud if possible.

Declaration was a normal part of worship in Old Testament times. Today, the various Christian traditions take different approaches, but most have occasions on which they 'declare' together as part of worship. A declaration may be as simple as 'The Lord is here', or celebratory, such as 'Alleluia! Christ is risen!' on Easter Sunday. It may be a psalm or another passage of scripture, or something designed for a particular occasion. When written records were scarce, songs were a vital way of declaring God's goodness, mercy and faithfulness and passing knowledge of him to future generations. Can you think of a hymn or song with this sense of declaration? (For example, 'We declare that the Kingdom of God is here' by Graham Kendrick.) Choose some words of declaration, from

Psalm 145 or elsewhere, to use at intervals today. If you can share them with others, all the better!

3. Read Luke 1:26–56.

Mary grew up in a community within which worshipping God and following his lead were not unusual. We'll be looking at her trusting obedience in the next chapter. For now, simply consider what this passage reveals about her and the clues it gives to the formative influences that had prepared her to be the mother of Jesus. Are you aware of the role God has for you and of the way he has been shaping you to fulfil it? Allow God time to speak to you about this.

5

TRUSTING OBEDIENCE

Trusting obedience is at the heart of discipleship. Jesus instructed his followers to 'go and make disciples of all nations… teaching them to obey everything I have commanded you' (Matthew 28:19–20). Obedience to Father God is intended to be the norm for us, as it was for Jesus—part of showing the family likeness (John 5:19; Matthew 12:50)—but how normal is it? Those who receive Christ as their Saviour may hear about baptism and the obligations of church membership, including tithing; they may be encouraged to share their newfound faith with friends and family; but… obeying all that Jesus commanded? Putting the Lord's will ahead of their own in day-to-day choices? John made it plain: 'This is love for God: to obey his commands. And his commands are not burdensome' (1 John 5:3). Try using that verse as a discussion starter and see where it takes you!

When Paul urged 'all those in Rome who are loved by God and called to be saints' (Romans 1:7) to be intentional about transformation, obedience was central to the picture he painted:

So here's what I want you to do, God helping you: Take your everyday, ordinary life—your sleeping, eating, going-to-work, and walking-around life—and place it before God as an offering.

Embracing what God does for you is the best thing you can do for him. Don't become so well-adjusted to your culture that you fit into it without even thinking. Instead, fix your attention on God. You'll be changed from the inside out. Readily recognise what he wants from you, and quickly respond to it. Unlike the culture around you, always dragging you down to its level of immaturity, God brings the best out of you, develops well-formed maturity in you.

ROMANS 12:1–2, *The Message*

Readily recognising what God wants and quickly responding to it is an excellent description of trusting obedience. Note also the ideas of being changed 'from the inside out' and being brought to greater maturity. As we obey God, we are being changed for the better.

I've linked obedience with the word 'trusting' not only to emphasise the positive spirit in which godly obedience is given but also to make a vital link with Chapter 2. Obeying a heavenly Father whom we love and trust can be a positive experience, even when we can't understand why he is sending us in a particular direction or asking us to do something he knows we find difficult or unpleasant.

For some people, it comes as a dreadful shock that they can't expect everything to be spelled out before making a move, but, as Oswald Chambers writes, 'You could read volumes on the work of the Holy Spirit, when five minutes of total, uncompromising obedience would make things as clear as sunlight.' Elaborating on the same theme, he says, 'The golden rule to follow to obtain spiritual understanding is not one of intellectual pursuit, but one of obedience… Intellectual darkness is the result of ignorance, but spiritual darkness is the result of something that I do not intend to obey' (*My Utmost for His Highest*, October 10, July 27). The Lord may reveal more as we obey, but sometimes, in his mercy, he shields us: if we saw our destination we might feel overwhelmed. Part of growing in relationship with him is learning that, while he can cope with our questions, he may ask us to carry on in trusting obedience while waiting for an answer.

It's tempting to assume that, if we obey God, his purposes for us will include being successful in terms of an identifiable, God-glorifying endpoint. This assumption overlooks the priority God gives to our becoming more like Jesus. Our learning to trust and obey in the challenges along the way, rather than relying on our own strategising, and to do so with a good grace, may be more significant in kingdom terms than wherever it was we thought we were heading.

'Yes, but...!'

Jesus taught his disciples to pray, 'Your Kingdom come, your will be done', words we pray readily enough. Yet, as the practicalities of doing God's will come into focus, there are difficulties, not least with our sinful nature. Even Paul, who had learned to live with expectant trust as a way of life, experienced frustration: 'I have the desire to do what is good, but I cannot carry it out' (Romans 7:18; read on into Romans 8 for more on the topic of our sinful nature).

A difficulty of a different kind is that the word 'obedience' has not travelled well through history. Let it reverberate around the theatre of your mind and notice the images presenting themselves. Are you flashing back to a particular setting or event, or to a particular person? What emotions are stirred? Obedience may have acquired negative associations, such as with threats ('You *will* obey me... or else...') or with misguided attempts to 'break your will' rather than teaching you to use it constructively.

Nowadays, obedience is often confused with compliance—for example, the sulky following of instructions by a petulant child. We do children a disservice if we teach them only to comply; while an explanation of the difference may be informative, what they really need is to see genuine obedience in action. If they are seeing those who love Jesus responding gladly to his will (John 15:14), they'll be learning what it means to obey with a trusting heart.

Seeing religious compliance in action, on the other hand, will be teaching them that, provided they stay within the lines outwardly, their inner life is of no interest to God. This is the 'painting-by-numbers' approach to obedience. Obeying God with a certain amount of precision, yet with a level of enthusiasm usually reserved for parking regulations, may 'tick the box' but it will have a pernicious effect on our relationship with him. You may find it helpful to pause and consider whether patterns of compliance from childhood relationships (overtly sulky or not) have been perpetuated in adult life. If so, they will be affecting relationships (at home or at work) and your ability to function effectively within the body of Christ.

Part of readying our hearts to obey God is allowing him to plant and develop, deep within us, a lively awareness that he is God and we are not. On a pragmatic level, if the God we worship and serve is worthy of the title 'The Almighty', this must mean he is able to see beyond whatever is currently overwhelming us. What's more, if we know him to be the God of love, following his lead makes sense. The reality is that our God is building his kingdom on a scale that we shall always find unimaginable (this side of heaven, at least). Trusting obedience will enable us not only to keep going and to play our part in challenging times now, but also to grow into the people he created us to be—ready and equipped to play even more of a part in due course.

So, with or without insight as to his purposes, are you prepared to press on to take hold of that for which Christ Jesus has taken hold of you (see Philippians 3:12b)? How about expressing your answer to God?

Choosing to yield

Jacob wrestled with God and received a blessing (Genesis 32:22–32), but I feel uneasy when this extraordinary passage is expounded to mean that resisting God is a route to blessing or is an aspect of godly perseverance. There's no doubt that it was a deeply significant encounter for Jacob, who, at that time, was given the name Israel. However, the collective wisdom of scripture and specific words of Jesus encourage us to yield to God.

Everyday images illustrate what it means to yield. For example, when negotiating roundabouts, wise drivers yield according to the rules that allow these features of the road to operate safely. More generally, we may yield to someone be-cause of their special expertise or superior physical strength, or because of their authority. A particularly vivid example is that of a drowning person, who needs to stop struggling and yield (willingly surrender) to the lifeguard's care and instructions.

Yielding to God's will means choosing to put aside our own. Yielding is character-forming, whether we're setting our hearts and minds 'on what the Spirit desires' (Romans 8:5) and yielding to God's will, yielding to someone else's will, yielding to others on the road or, indeed, yielding to temptation. Each time we yield to temptation, it becomes easier: the dynamic of being 'changed from the inside out' is in operation but is no longer bringing 'the best out of' us and 'developing well-formed maturity' (Romans 12:2, THE MESSAGE). Yielding to temptation means yielding to the will of the one who, from the beginning, has been casting doubt upon God's goodness and his concern for our well-being. This has consequences not simply in terms of the acts committed but in terms of choosing darkness rather than light. You could pause and ask God to bring to mind any recent occasion on which you have yielded to temptation. If he does so, why not ask for his forgiveness and cleansing before continuing?

Jesus likened the man who came to him, heard what he had to say and put it into practice to the wise house-builder who dug down deep and laid foundations on rock. We looked at this in Chapter 1, but I mention it again here because many of us have a tendency to debate, negotiate and bargain with God. Instead of entrusting ourselves to his will, we'd rather bring him round to ours. While he is telling us the way to go, we are scanning the horizon for more palatable options and devising suitably holy-sounding arguments to justify them. Well, there certainly are a variety of other ways to live life, but Jesus likened them to building on sand (Matthew 7:24–26). 'Why do you call me, "Lord, Lord," and do not do what I say?'(Luke 6:46). That's still a good question to ponder.

Embracing God's purposes

God isn't just looking for trusting obedience over specific decisions on particular occasions. Trusting obedience is to be our way of life—aligning our will with his will, continually choosing to yield at heart level. This will affect the way we think and feel as well as our visible actions. Regrettably, in today's consumer culture, 'choosing' has become almost synonymous with 'pleasing myself'. Many liberated men and women find it strange to think of voluntarily yielding to anyone, let alone to God. But if we're willing to choose yielding to God as a way of life, God may use us in ways that we'd have been sure were beyond us.

I don't know what Mary was doing when the angel arrived, but it must have been a shock for her (Luke 1:29). 'Do not be afraid, Mary,' said Gabriel, 'you have found favour with God. You will be with child and give birth to a son, and you are to give him the name Jesus. He will be great and will be called the Son of the Most High. The Lord God will give him the throne of his father David, and he will reign over the house of Jacob for ever; his kingdom will never end' (vv. 30–33). Imagine Mary, probably a teenager, trying to take it all in. She hasn't begun to grapple with the idea of a king whose reign will surpass anything seen in her nation. Her attention has

been grabbed by something earlier in the conversation: 'Er...
hold on, did you say "*baby*"?'

We're familiar with Gabriel's explanation of the Holy
Spirit coming upon her and God's power bringing about
a conception in a truly miraculous way (vv. 35–37), but
I wonder what it was like for Mary to hear it. For a start,
she'd have known the consequences of having a baby out of
wedlock; that much was clear, even if she hadn't processed
the rest. Yet, faced with potentially life-threatening and certainly life-changing circumstances, her heart was ready. Her
response, 'I am the Lord's servant. May it be to me as you
have said' (v. 38) should be heard not as 'OK, whatever' but
as willing receptivity: 'I can't understand how it's going to
work out, but I trust you and I choose to serve you.'

Trusting obedience such as this doesn't come out of
the blue: Mary knew God's character. She'd had years of
absorbing godly values, living according to his will among
women and men who did the same, and had no doubt
learned to yield to him in less challenging circumstances.
From an early age, Mary would have heard story after story
of God's faithful provision (see her song, which follows in
verses 46–55). She'd arrived at a settled position of trust,
which enabled her to embrace God's purposes for her life,
to follow when she didn't know where she was heading—or
feared that she *did* know.

I preached on this passage at a time when our church
family had been shaken repeatedly by serious illness and
untimely death. There seemed to be more bad news each
time we gathered. I was speaking in place of someone
whose baby grandchild had just died in circumstances that

had provoked allegations amid the shock and grief. Mary's response to the angel's message spoke to me and, I gather, to others at this time of pain and turmoil. We had the benefit of real live 'visual aids' among us—men and women showing trusting obedience while coping with family tragedy and life-threatening conditions. In this context, God used Mary's story to challenge the rest of us about our character development. Had we been prayerfully living according to God's will, absorbing godly values from the scriptures, developing the capacities and resilience needed for what lay ahead? You might like to ask yourself the same question.

Yielding to others?

Walking with Christ and becoming more like him will involve building healthy relationships with others. The lie we are fed by 'the father of lies' (John 8:44) is that it's not possible to do both. It *is* possible, but Jesus taught that 'no one can serve two masters' (Matthew 6:24). So, as Jesus' disciples, we must be clear about who's in charge.

Many of us encounter the question 'Who's in charge?' daily in the workplace. If we're under contract to an employer, letting them set our pattern of work and obeying their instructions is likely to come under the heading of 'godly living'. We may sense that Jesus is with us as we occasionally go the extra mile for them, but serious questions are in order if the extra mile becomes a daily marathon or if there's pressure to act in ungodly ways. We cannot allow this to go unchallenged and then plead, 'I was only doing my job.' Even if alternatives are few and all seem equally risky, God is good and faithful, so yielding to his will is safer than it may feel. Is there an issue of yielding in your workplace or elsewhere that you need to bring to God?

Family and intimate relationships also bring dilemmas. For example, God commands us to honour our parents (Exodus 20:12), but how much yielding should this involve? The sense that we've found Mr or Miss Right may bring pressure to yield to another's will. Marriage, pregnancy and children all bring challenges. For some, however, the arrival of grandchildren is 'the big one'! I enjoy spending time with mine, and with their parents, but I'm alarmed by the extent to which some of my contemporaries' lives have been hijacked. Grandparents can be a tremendous source of blessing to families but, if their lives start to revolve around the needs and preferences of the younger generations to the exclusion of all else, there will be consequences. It's not only a problem for the grandparents, whose relationship with God will be tested and perhaps strained or weakened. It's also a formative influence on the younger generations: if Granny and Gramps are failing to reveal any evidence of their higher calling—that God has first claim on their affections—they're selling the much-loved little ones short.

The scriptures tell us to serve one another in love, and loving and serving will include taking account of the preferences of others, but there's wisdom in bringing before God all relationships in which we make a habit of yielding. He may want to pinpoint areas within them that are outside his will, including in relationships that are part of our service for him. It's good to visualise ourselves standing upright before God—with others, yes, but not bent towards them in a deforming posture that inclines us away from our heavenly Father. We serve others, but as part of following Jesus, the servant-king.

If what you have read has raised concerns about a relationship, it could be fruitful to air your thoughts with a praying friend as a sounding-board. If it's possible that yielding to others has taken you outside God's will, you may have to tell him you're ready to repent before you're able to see things clearly. The key is to seek God and to ask for his perspective; to look up and out of the relationship rather than simply scrutinising the relationship itself. You'll need to ask God's forgiveness if a relationship has taken you in sinful directions and shaped you (and maybe also others) in ungodly ways.

Oh no, not 'discipline'!

Sooner or later, all Jesus' apprentices have to confront their feelings about discipline, another word that has not travelled well through history. For some, it's inextricably linked with punishment—not helped by those who use the words as if their meanings were identical. They're not! Healthy discipline is designed to make punishment unnecessary. For example, a footballer who binges before a game and turns up unfit to play will be punished, perhaps by a fine. He has acted in breach of disciplines associated with fitness and match preparation, and the whole team has suffered. The disciplines were put in place for a reason; punishment is one of the possible consequences of neglecting them.

Here is a different picture. When I provide a trellis for my clematis plant and, from time to time, entwine a few more tendrils so that it may progress upwards, I'm disciplining it, not punishing it. The trellis provides stability, making the clematis less likely to be battered down by wind and rain. I keep the plant in contact with the trellis because I want it to become all that a clematis can be. An undisciplined clematis in a heap on the ground is not only less able to benefit from the sunlight and display its glory, it's also at the mercy of slugs and passing boots. I'm disciplining it for its own good.

If, in the past, you've been crushed while being told 'It's for your own good', you may need to ask God for courage to let him into the tender places. It could be helpful to have a healing prayer counsellor alongside as you allow God to touch and heal your wounds. Although journeys towards receiving healing have many steps, some of them painful, they're worth it because healing allows us to become more completely the men and women God created us to be. In the case of wounds from the ungodly actions of others done in the name of 'discipline', healing will open the way to practising trusting obedience and entering more fully into all that it means to be a disciple.

Before going on to look at self-discipline, a few words about what discipline (from self or others) cannot do. First, it's not a cure for inner brokenness, any more than marathon training is a cure for a broken leg. A sensible athlete chooses a healthy diet while waiting for an injury to heal and, while inner healing is taking place, spiritual disciplines (more on these later) will help with 'nutrition'. We need healing for our brokenness and, to find it, we must turn to God himself. A determination to hold it all together unaided will get in the way of what God wants to do. Second, discipline is not a remedy for sin. Once we've repented and received forgiveness, God may highlight particular disciplines that will help us break patterns of sinful behaviour, but the only remedy for sin is the one that God has already provided through Christ our Saviour. We can't discipline ourselves into a DIY 'solution'.

Self-discipline

It's regrettable that some people see all attempts to exhort God's children to discipline themselves as sidelining grace and devaluing the work of the Holy Spirit. Stackhouse is clear: 'To think one can survive simply on a diet of pietistic enthusiasm without intense discipline is like a budding pianist thinking she can perform in the concert halls of the world without serious practice.' His view is that 'our fear of Pharisaism is precisely what is keeping us from fleshing out a faith that will really cut it with the world' (*The Day is Yours*, p. 136). Encouragingly, Paul describes self-discipline as a gift from God—one of the many which are ours to take up and use as we follow Christ (2 Timothy 1:7, NIV; 'calm *and* well-balanced mind *and* discipline *and* self-control', Amplified Bible). Are we as ready to receive this gift as God is to give it?

Our English word 'discipline' comes from the Latin *disciplina*, which is the instruction given to *discipuli*—apprentices, pupils, disciples. Discipline from parents and teachers is intended to provide direction and a supportive outer structure for inner growth and character development, much like the trellis that guides and supports the clematis. In the case of children, however, the aim is that external structures and guidance might decrease in influence with time. Youngsters need to learn *self*-discipline, so that they may grow into adults who know the wisdom of going to bed at an appropriate hour, setting the alarm in order to be ready for work, and so on.

Paul likened the Christian life to a race (for example, 1 Corinthians 9:24–25; Galatians 5:7; see also Hebrews 12:1), so let's see what we may learn from the parallels. Imagine two athletes participating in the London Marathon. Bill has trained faithfully throughout the winter, taking advice from more experienced athletes and constructing a plan designed to have him race-ready on the day. Fred began with good intentions but allowed winter weather to keep him rooted to the sofa, relying on the exercise of opening the fridge now and then. Bill and Fred will run the same route but their experiences of the race will be poles apart. What's more, the event will 'form' them differently as athletes. It may shape their overall futures very differently, too.

We accept that, for sporting activities, the self-discipline, pain and sheer inconvenience of a training regime are necessary preparation for the challenges ahead. What about in our spiritual 'race'? This race is intended to be run as a team, urging one another on, including during the periods of training. Of course, in life, it may be difficult to work out what constitutes the training and what is the real event. When a major crisis slams into us, it feels like the only event in our lives. Often, it's only in retrospect that we see the training value of the difficulties—how they've been used by God as his instruments of transformation.

As followers of Jesus seeking to become more like him, is it possible to 'overtrain'? I don't believe it is, if we really are letting him lead. The problem is that those who are overtired and overstretched may not discern his leading accurately. Also, some are driven by their own needs to engage in struggles that are not part of God's plan, sacrificing themselves (and maybe also their families) in ways that undermine rather than serve God's purposes. We're all capable of making unwise decisions and of meeting our needs in unhealthy ways; it's good to watch out for one another. If a brother or sister in Christ seems to be accumulating 'to do' lists or filling their diary rather than building godly character, or if they're focusing on religious activities while losing touch with Jesus and the people close to them, this is cause for concern.

'Loose' thoughts and emotions?

Paul wrote to the Corinthians, 'We use our powerful God-tools for smashing warped philosophies, tearing down barriers erected against the truth of God, fitting every loose thought and emotion and impulse into the structure of life shaped by Christ. Our tools are ready at hand for clearing the ground of every obstruction and building lives of obedience into maturity' (2 Corinthians 10:5–6, THE MESSAGE; see also Romans 12:2).

It's vital to include our thought-life when considering self-discipline, because some who are willing to follow guidelines for behaviour seem to believe they are free to entertain whatever thoughts they wish—well, except on Sundays, perhaps! In his Sermon on the Mount, Jesus taught that our thought-life is important. (This is the context in which he named lustful thoughts as adultery of the heart: Matthew 5:28.) There is no doubt that dwelling on thoughts about particular behaviours is not only formative but also makes those behaviours more likely to be enacted (James 1:13–15 is relevant here).

Even if ungodly thoughts aren't acted upon, giving them 'house room' makes the Spirit of Jesus less welcome. Imagine asking him to stand outside for half an hour to allow some 'private time' with our thoughts. How daft does that sound? Rather, let's invite Jesus to make himself more at home. We could welcome the Holy Spirit's inspiration and mull over how best to bring blessing to those we love or how best to serve our community—making *these* behaviours more likely to be enacted. Also, rather than engaging in one of those interminable arguments (with ourselves or others) about whether something is or is not permissible for a child of God living by grace, we could simply ask, 'Can I see myself doing this and then chatting happily to Jesus about it afterwards?'

In an age in which feelings have been given a new prominence and authority, we must lift high the truth that we are not helplessly at the mercy of our moods and emotions. Some thoughts, if entertained, have a predictable effect. If, for example, when faced with difficult circumstances, I chew endlessly on the idea that God has forgotten me and that no one cares, my mood will be adversely affected. Alternatively, I could choose to feed my mind a diet of grace and truth. I'd still feel sadness or other emotions related to the difficulties, and I might still need to seek God for healing for wounds received, but I wouldn't be propelling myself into a downward spiral. This choosing can be literally life-saving.

I have no wish to imply that feelings are 'bad' or to be done away with: they're not. They're like children—all the better for being held within a secure framework ('the structure of a life shaped by Christ') and educated rather than being allowed to run riot or put in charge of major decisions. (I'm grateful to Lin Button for this way of visualising feelings.) As much-loved children of God, we're wise if we listen to our heavenly Father and to voices speaking grace and truth, not just to how we feel—or, indeed, to how others feel.

You could pause and bring into consciousness the thoughts and emotions that have been stirred while you've been reading about discipline and self-discipline. Which points made sense? Did some go against teaching you've absorbed or challenge attitudes you've formed? If you feel disturbed, why not bring this disturbance to God, asking for his protection and for discernment as you read on?

Spiritual disciplines

The term 'spiritual disciplines' will be unfamiliar to some, but they are nothing new. The list includes prayer, worship, Bible study, serving and fellowship. Dallas Willard's book, *The Spirit of the Disciplines*, and Richard Foster's *Celebration of Discipline* are recommended reading for all who would like to be taken through the relevant biblical material, which is too extensive to cover adequately here.

Rueben Job explains the role of the disciplines like this:

Spiritual disciplines keep us in that healing, redeeming presence and power of God that forms and transforms each of us more and more into the image of the One we seek to follow. We… must find

our way of living and practising those disciplines that will keep us in love with God—practices that will help keep us positioned in such a way that we may hear and be responsive to God's slightest whisper of direction and receive God's promised presence and power every day and in every situation.
THREE SIMPLE RULES, PP. 54–55

It's not all plain sailing, though. For some people, unease over spiritual disciplines comes from having encountered them as graceless impositions within a heavy authority structure. Others have seen them misused in futile, grace-denying attempts to earn salvation (often called 'works': see Ephesians 2:8–9). Some have questioned whether it's even possible for spiritual disciplines to have a place in the lives of those who worship and serve the God of grace. To clarify: we are saved by grace and there is nothing we can do to earn our salvation. Here, nothing really does mean nothing—nothing at all, ever. Yet scripture also calls us to 'work out what God has worked in' (see, for example, Philippians 2:12–13). As Dallas Willard has underlined on numerous occasions in writing and in speaking, grace is opposed to works, but it is not opposed to effort. Willard explains that 'once the spirit comes alive in God, the lengthy processes of subduing all aspects of the self under God can begin. This is the process of spiritual formation' (*Renovation of the Heart*, p. 41).

Billy Graham told a story about a man who raced his sled dogs each week. He placed his bets differently, but he always won. 'How do you do it?' the villagers eventually asked. 'Well, I know which dogs I've fed and trained this week, and which I haven't,' he replied. You could ask yourself, 'Which habits and attitudes have I been starving, and which have I been feeding this week?'

This is where spiritual disciplines come in—not as a way of bullying an unregenerate life into a shape that will pass muster for two hours on a Sunday, much as a Sergeant Major might work on a recruit who's been disgracing the regiment on parade. The disciplines are for those of us who have already been born again, who are glad to have been 'redeemed from the empty way of life' handed down to us (1 Peter 1:18). They're gifts from God to help us appropriate more fully the grace we've already received. Furthermore, each spiritual discipline brings with it a corresponding freedom: they serve as weedkiller to the habits remaining from our former life that need putting to death (Colossians 3:5–10). Under God's hand, the disciplines tend our hearts, as we might tend a garden, making them more congenial places for Jesus to inhabit.

When somebody starts to follow Jesus, we could encourage them to ask the question, 'What kind of spiritual nourishment do I need so that Jesus' life in me will grow stronger and become more pervasive?' The same question is also relevant for those of us who have been apprenticed to the Master for rather longer. If our diet is limited to 'five a day'—five 'God-minutes' shoe-horned into an otherwise unreflective life—we're probably not growing very fast (Hebrews 5:13—6:2 is relevant here).

The spiritual discipline of reading and meditating on the Bible regularly may seem nothing more than a habit—a good habit, of course (2 Timothy 3:16–17). Yet each morning, by means of this discipline, I (and countless others) say to God, 'Tell me more.' Then, when the Holy Spirit brings the scriptures alive to my heart, I take in life-affirming truth and receive life-sustaining grace. Reading the Gospels, I encounter the authentic Jesus. If part of my life is not under his Lordship, this area is thrown into sharp relief. Seeing a concern through the lens of scripture brings insight and direction, or at least a sense that 'God is able'.

I find Jesus' teaching on the discipline of fasting particularly penetrating in Eugene Peterson's version: 'When you practice some appetite-denying discipline to better concentrate on God, don't make a production out of it. It might turn you into a small-time celebrity but it won't make you a saint. If you "go into training" inwardly, act normal outwardly. Shampoo and comb your hair, brush your teeth, wash your face' (Matthew 6:16–18, *THE MESSAGE*). His advice not to 'make a production out of it' may be applied to all the disciplines: their purpose is to welcome God's nourishing of the Christ-life in us, not to advertise our spirituality. Why not think of a discipline that is familiar to you and reflect on how your heavenly Father has been using it in your life?

Trusting obedience is good for us

I have long been drawn to Jesus' words at the end of Matthew 11, which begin, 'Come to me, all you who are weary and burdened, and I will give you rest' (v. 28). They're often preached as a personal invitation from Jesus to a weary follower, and no doubt those who have turned to him as a result have found blessing. But the context shows that, when Jesus spoke them in the first century, there were additional layers of meaning.

The surrounding chapters in this Gospel paint a picture of increasing conflict and opposition. Jesus had responded to John the Baptist's enquiry, 'Are you the one…?' (11:3) by pointing to actions confirming his identity as Messiah. He'd denounced cities that had ignored his authenticating miracles, comparing Capernaum unfavourably with Sodom (11:23–24). Then we see Jesus on a collision course with the Pharisees over sabbath observance, saying, 'There is far more at stake here than religion. If you had any idea what this Scripture meant—"I prefer a flexible heart to an inflexible ritual"—you wouldn't be nitpicking like this' (12:6–7, *THE MESSAGE*).

Into this powderkeg context, Jesus speaks his powerful, life-saving invitation: 'Come to me… learn from me.' It's inescapable that Jesus is offering a working relationship, an opportunity for apprentices to discover in the company of the Master how to live life to the full. When I hear Jesus' words 'Come to me and find rest' used merely as an invitation to take some time out before returning to the fray ('back to the treadmill'), I am dismayed. This was never an invitation to 'take time out': Jesus was urging his hearers to leave their current way of living, *never to return*! And the 'rest' isn't what many mean when they think of 'having a rest', either.

I said near the end of my first book, subtitled 'Discovering the rhythms of grace' (reflecting *THE MESSAGE* version of Jesus' words):

The picture is of learning to follow the pace and direction of God's steps within an intimate relationship, rather than on working through a list of instructions. The pace he sets for us will take account of our humanity; it may sometimes stretch us, but it will

not harm us. It will vary from season to season in our lives, but will never become frenzied—neither will it grind to a halt... it's rest yoked to Jesus, going at his pace and in his direction—not the rest of enforced inactivity.
DRIVEN BEYOND THE CALL OF GOD, P. 198

Jesus has invited us to walk with him and to watch how he does things, to practise 'trusting obedience' all day, every day. The expectation is that, over time, this will be formative. What's more, finding soul rest will be restorative, good for our health and for the well-being of those around us. If it ever catches on, it could be good for the Church, too!

One way of responding to this chapter would be to pray, 'Your kingdom come, your will be done' at regular intervals over the next week or so, elaborating on these phrases as your heart is led. You could, if you're ready, pray, 'Lord, teach me to trust and obey.' Before doing so, though, make sure you're prepared for the training opportunities God may well send in response.

THE FRUIT OF THE SPIRIT

When Paul was writing to the Galatians, the Greek word *prautes*, translated 'gentleness', brought together thoughts not only of humility but also of strength under control (the real meaning of the word 'meekness'). Today, the presence of strength is less likely to be acknowledged by this word, which some associate with being wishy-washy or spineless. Yet gentleness means the opposite of 'losing it' (as in 'He was so rude about my competition entry that I just lost it—I told him what he could do with his expertise'). Jesus showed how to be angry without losing control (for example, see Mark 3:5). Gentle people have the strength of character to remain pleasantly courteous while correcting those who are in error (2 Timothy 2:25) and, when appropriate, expressing anger. So much for being spineless!

In the Old Testament, we find this gentle humility associated with being teachable (Psalm 25:9) and with a promise of seeing God's goodness in the days to come (for example, Psalm 37:11; 149:4). Zechariah foresaw the righteous saviour-king, 'gentle and riding on a donkey, on a colt, the foal of a donkey' (Zechariah 9:9; see also Matthew 21:1–11). Jesus fulfilled this prophecy of a gentle saviour in his daily life, not just in the manner of his arrival in Jerusalem. In Matthew 11:29, he invites us to learn from him, adding, 'for I am gentle and humble in heart, and you will find rest for your souls'.

In my experience, gentle people can be very restful to be with. There's no need to watch my back or to choose words carefully lest they overreact to the way it all tumbles out—a real gift in an edgy world. Can you think of someone you know who is gentle, and identify why you think of them in this way? Thank God for them and, if you know that Christ-like gentleness has yet to emerge as a feature of your character, how about asking that same person to pray for you?

In his letters, Paul is upfront about his desire for Christians to demonstrate Christ's transforming influence as communities, not just as individuals: 'Be completely humble and gentle; be patient, bearing with one another in love. Make every effort to keep the unity of the Spirit through the bond of peace' (Ephesians 4:2–3). In James' list of characteristics of 'the wisdom that comes from heaven', the adjective derived from *prautes* is translated 'considerate' (James 3:17). Remaining united at heart-level and being considerate towards one another through the ups and downs of church life takes lots of 'bearing with one another in love'. But this speaks volumes to people outside, especially those who've forgotten what it's like *not* to have to walk on eggshells and those needing a safe place to rest their world-weary souls. When praying for your church and its impact on the wider community, these verses could be a conduit for inspiration.

Now, by way of contrast, imagine a litter of newborn puppies on a slippery floor. There's plenty of energetic scrabbling but, until they learn greater control, effort is wasted. Once they get the hang of it, they'll be able to come when their master calls. Until they do, they'll illustrate what we're like before the Holy Spirit has brought to birth in us the self-control (*egkrateia*; 'temperance', KJV) necessary to enjoy directing our energies towards God's purposes.

Self-control is also central to one of Peter's lists:

Make every effort to add to your faith goodness; and to goodness, knowledge; and to knowledge, self-control; and to self-control, perseverance; and to perseverance, godliness; and to godliness, brotherly kindness; and to brotherly kindness, love. For if you possess these qualities in increasing measure, they will keep you from being ineffective and unproductive in your knowledge of our Lord Jesus Christ.

2 PETER 1:5–8

Ceasing to follow every impulse or physical desire, and refusing to live at the mercy of turbulent emotions, we come to a place where we're able to surrender our energies and passions to Jesus' direction—and to delight in the fruit he brings forth in our lives as a result.

Without self-control, we are not only ineffective and unproductive; we're also vulnerable (Proverbs 25:28). In the second half of the 19th century, a temperance movement called the Band of Hope became active in the United Kingdom. My grandmother was among those who 'took the pledge' to avoid alcohol. These days, similar movements encourage teenagers to maintain sexual purity. Also, men and women struggling with particular temptations have the option of joining the relevant 'Anonymous' group—for example, 'Gamblers Anonymous'. While welcoming the Holy Spirit's transforming influence on our self-control, there's real gain in admitting, 'I have a problem.' In so doing, we see truth opening the door to grace. In practical terms, there is also much to be gained from being accountable to those who are already familiar with all the usual tales told to 'justify' lapses.

For Jesus' disciples, self-control is essential in everyday matters, too—for example, in choosing not to be provoked and 'engaging brain before opening mouth'. The tongue is often the last part of the body to be mastered (James 3:2–12). We may pray words from one of David's psalms: 'Set a guard over my mouth, O Lord; keep watch over the door of my lips' (Psalm 141:3).

In closing this section, I'd like to underline that God-inspired self-control is not joyless. Pause for a moment and review what has been going through your mind while reading the paragraphs above. Self-control is often narrowly portrayed as relating only to 'don'ts', to past failures and struggles to come. How often have you thanked God for the delight to be found in well-directed energies and fruitfulness? If you missed this on your first reading, why not reread the section, asking God to redraw your internal picture of self-control? Are you ready to invite him to form this aspect of Jesus' character in you?

BIBLE REFLECTIONS

1. Read Jeremiah 18:1–6.

In her song 'Jesus, You are changing me', Marilyn Baker uses the imagery of a potter working with clay, and asks the Lord to help her to be willing to be shaped by him. Ask yourself: 'Do I trust God enough to invite him to mould and shape me, now and in the days to come?' We're not passive clay; we may be tempted to give the Potter instructions or set limits on how far he may go. Pain or fear may make it difficult to yield to God's hands, but we may ask for courage. Might it be possible to learn to enjoy being shaped by God rather than fearing what he might do? If you have access to clay or another modelling material, you could make something while talking to him about the feelings this reflection has evoked.

2. Read Matthew 14.

Imagine being one of Jesus' followers, with these events unfolding around you. Note when Jesus is close by and when he's at a distance. As you hear about the murder of Jesus' relative and the foolishness surrounding it, how are you expecting Jesus to respond? How *does* he respond? Later, in the middle of nowhere with lots of tired and hungry people, someone makes a sensible suggestion (v. 15). How do you feel about Jesus' response? (See vv. 16, 18; try not to edit your feelings, knowing how it all turns out.)

You spend an exhausting day, then face more challenges after dark: visualise the churning sea; feel the spray, the wind, the cold and the fear. Jesus describes Peter's faith as tiny—yet Peter is the one who had the courage to trust and step out of the boat.

Come back to today's circumstances. Is there disturbing news to be faced? A major undertaking to be seen through with seemingly inadequate resources? A call to follow the Master into unfamiliar territory? The challenges will be different from those faced by Jesus' first disciples, but there may be principles he wants you to draw from the passage. Listen for his words of reassurance as you choose to trust him over the next few weeks.

3. Read Luke 5:1–11 and John 21:1–6.

We see Peter first at the start of his discipleship and then immediately before he is recommissioned by his resurrected Lord (having denied him). Peter, an experienced fisherman, has done what non-fisherman Jesus told him to do, with amazing results. Why do you think Peter followed Jesus' instructions? Carry these two episodes from Peter's life in your mind for a few days. Is it possible that God may have something to offer in your areas of competence at work, or in other areas of life in which you're happy that you know what you're doing? Trusting obedience could bring unexpected fruitfulness in your work or your family life this week.

6

FRUIT THAT WILL LAST

Whether in the garden, the orchard or the polytunnel, fruit-bearing takes time. In the United Kingdom, most people come into contact with fruit only when it's ready to eat; years of nurture preparing trees or vines for fruiting, and the labour in the months leading up to each picking season, are largely out of sight and mind. Those to whom the scriptures about fruit and fruitfulness were originally addressed were much more aware of the time and care involved in producing any harvest. They might well have suffered hardship due to crop failure and would have understood the need to nurture plants towards fruitfulness.

If you live in a town or city, you could study the range of fruit and vegetables available, and take time to be thankful, next time you're shopping. Alternatively, think of the most luscious harvest festival display imaginable. Visualise the array of colours and the different shapes, sizes and textures. Call to mind the scents of fruit and flowers, flowing together into a full-bodied aroma. Pause to thank God for what the scene represents. Now consider this: seasonal fruit is incredibly short-lived, but God makes it beautiful. Let's keep this in mind as we approach the long-lasting fruit we are to bear—fruit that will call forth praise to his name, fruit that will contribute to our spreading everywhere 'the fragrance of the knowledge of him… the aroma of Christ' (2 Corinthians 2:14–15).

When Christians talk about 'bearing fruit' today, it's often in the context of 'saving souls'. Our thoughts may leap to well-known evangelists such as Billy Graham, leaving most of us feeling inadequate—but what about Albert McMakin, whom God used to bring the young Billy to hear Jesus' invitation? The fruit of Albert's willingness to respond to God's leading has been multiplied millions of times in the years since that day. However, there's much more to fruitfulness than 'bringing others to Christ'. That's not to diminish the importance of sharing our faith (and let none of what follows be taken to mean anything of the sort), but, as bearing fruit is such a vast subject, I'll be concentrating on aspects of particular relevance to ground already covered in this book.

Expectations

Gardeners know about cultivation: for example, plants, shrubs and trees that are fed and watered according to their needs are more resistant to disease and much more likely to produce a good crop. In the spiritual realm, God has made available a rich supply of all that is necessary for growth, resistance to 'disease', and fruitfulness. Yet many followers of Jesus have been conditioned to expect little fruit, so they shrug, sigh and muddle on. The thinking goes something like this: 'As we're sinners, we shouldn't expect too much; we just have to be thankful that God is gracious and willing to use even people like us.'

This way of thinking needs challenging because it has serious, far-reaching, grace-denying consequences. Low expectations become normative: 'There's no point in dwelling on the disappointment; let's just make the best of how it is.' This attitude sidelines God's fully resourced plan for us to be living Christ-revealing lives, full of grace and truth, and there's no doubt that it hinders the extension of God's kingdom rule. Mahatma Gandhi, for example, studied the scriptures and was attracted to Christ's teaching, yet in the behaviour of those who called themselves 'Christians' he found a disturbing level of incongruity. Gandhi is widely quoted as saying that 'we would all become Christians' if Christians lived as Christ has taught them to live.

In a slightly adapted version of the old management adage, 'The belief system you have is perfectly designed to produce the results you are getting.' The world is being deprived of Christ-revealing lives, and God's children are being robbed of their promised 'life to the full' (John 10:10) on the basis that, well, it couldn't really be *that* good, especially in *your* case, could it? 'Did God really say…?' Yes, he did! He said he wanted us to bear fruit that would last, abide, remain, not spoil—and bring him glory (John 15:8, 16).

Some people struggle with the idea of being called to bear fruit; instead they settle for being useful. 'Useful' is good (as long as it doesn't slide into being 'used', which carries with it the sense of being manipulated to meet the needs or wants of others). And 'useful to God'—surely that has to be good? Well, yes and no. For a start, unlike usefulness, fruitfulness necessitates connectedness to God. Jesus spoke of this in terms of being part of the same vine. In God's scheme of things, he added, living a disconnected life brings not *less* fruit but *no* fruit (John 15:5). Paul put it this way: 'We take our lead from Christ, who is the source of everything we do… His very breath and blood flow through us, nourishing us so that we will grow up healthy in God, robust in love' (Ephesians 4:16, *THE MESSAGE*). Fruitfulness requires God's life flowing through us; a willingness to be used isn't enough.

A dustpan and brush are very useful; I don't know where I would be without mine. Yet too many Christians are happy to be kept busy, serving as God's dustpan and brush or something similarly utilitarian, when all the time he's looking for those who will inherit spiritual riches and manifest his family likeness. We're all called to serve: our serving is an expression of our relationship with the servant-king. But we serve as 'family', those who share 'DNA' and so much more, not as inanimate objects (useful but without the capacity for relationship). This is another example of low expectations being fulfilled: we risk being robbed of so much of what we were created to be.

Much-loved child of God, if you know you usually come to the Father to hear his 'to do' list rather than to sense his heart and be drawn deeper into his life, how about taking time now to hear what he has to say to you?

The principle of sowing and reaping

The scriptures refer to sowing and reaping, and this principle deserves attention. It's not a 'law' in the sense that the law of gravity is a law; God is gracious and full of mercy and we don't always get what we deserve. Jesus died for us while we were still sinners (Romans 5:7–8): what better illustration of God's grace and mercy? (It's also true that godly people sometimes suffer in ways that defy explanation.) But the principle of sowing and reaping sets out the way things generally work in God's world: it matters what a person sows and where he or she sows it. God has given us free will, and our choices have consequences for us, and usually also for others. Specifically in relation to fruitfulness, the choices we make affect the 'soil quality' of our hearts and thereby the potential for God's seed to flourish in us (Matthew 13:23).

The principle of sowing and reaping has applied since the earliest times. The Bible is packed with examples— sadly, many of them showing the misery that comes from scattering the spiritual equivalent of herbicide and reaping real-life desolation and disaster. The writer of Proverbs put the negative and positive aspects succinctly: 'A life devoted to things is a dead life, a stump; a God-shaped life is a flourishing tree' (11:28, THE MESSAGE).

In the New Testament, Paul expresses the same principle:

Don't be misled: no one makes a fool of God. What a person plants, he will harvest. The person who plants selfishness, ignoring the needs of others—ignoring God!—harvests a crop of weeds. All he'll have to show for his life is weeds! But the one who plants in response to God, letting God's Spirit do the growth work in him, harvests a crop of real life, eternal life.

GALATIANS 6:7–8, THE MESSAGE

In an age in which it is becoming increasingly acceptable to dodge responsibility for the consequences of our actions, we need to be wary of allowing cultural influences, rather than the scriptures, to shape our thinking.

Pruning and fruitfulness

The key passage on this aspect of fruitfulness is John 15:1–17. I recommend that, if possible, you read it before continuing. These verses make it crystal clear that, once our spiritual heredity is settled, God still has work to do in us. Followers of Jesus bearing fruit for his kingdom will experience pruning as a recurring event; we can't tick the 'no pruning' box when we sign up. I understand that there's a play on words in the Greek, which emphasises that the branch will either be 'cut off' or 'cut back'. I don't particularly enjoy being 'cut back' but, faced with the alternative of being 'cut off', I know which I would prefer.

In Jesus' day, the pruning of vines was seen as 'cleansing' them ('purging', KJV), and Jesus' words in verse 3 about his disciples already being 'clean' are linked to this idea. God the Father, the gardener (or vine-dresser), cuts off every non-fruiting branch and prunes fruitful branches (v. 2). Expert pruning often takes away wood that appears healthy and productive. We have to trust that the Master Gardener knows which stems are susceptible to disease and which will grow in unhelpful ways, impairing the fruiting capacity of the branch as a whole. This process is uncomfortable, but *it is not punishment*. It's done by the unerring hand of the God who is love, who can already see the enduring fruit that will result from his intervention.

Take a moment to speak out to God your response to these thoughts about pruning and purging. If they scare you, or you've always seen them as punishment, you could ask the Master Gardener to bring reassurance. If you know you've resisted being 'cut back', confess this to your loving heavenly Father. Ask his forgiveness and ask for courage and renewed strength to use in cooperating with his good purposes. Take time to listen to what God has to say to you about it all.

Spiritual heredity and fruit

These days, computer manipulation of images can make the impossible appear possible but, if I displayed pictures of blackberry bushes bearing apples, and runner beans sprouting from a fir tree, you'd have no hesitation in calling them fakes. The nature of each bush or tree determines the type of fruit it bears (Luke 6:44). The same is true of spiritual heredity and spiritual fruit. Jesus antagonised some of his contemporaries by commenting on such matters (John 8:31–59). As descendants of Abraham, they were satisfied with their pedigree but Jesus challenged them about their attitudes and actions, which, he said, revealed a different spiritual parentage.

Why not ask God to show you what your attitudes and actions have been revealing in recent days? Taking time for this could be very fruitful—and there's no pressing need to rush on to finish the book. Confess to God as necessary, receive his forgiveness (1 John 1:9), and don't come under condemnation. Then ask God to show you if there is anything that needs putting right with another person.

In addition to expecting trees and bushes to bring forth fruit according to their nature, we expect their seed to have the potential to bring into being more of the same; this has been so since the very beginning. Likewise, we who have received God's 'seed' (Greek: *sperma*) and allowed it (the spiritual equivalent of DNA) to remain and grow in us (1 John 3:9–10) may expect to go on to bear 'kingdom fruit'.

If we know we've been 'redeemed from the empty way of life' handed down to us by our forefathers (1 Peter 1:18), yet we are bringing forth no fruit at all in keeping with having God's seed in us, having the mind of Christ and so on, there's a problem. If you're concerned about your fruitfulness, I strongly recommend reviewing this chapter before God with a prayerful friend. Might the lack of fruit be related to accommodating other 'seed' in your heart? Is it possible that you've been watering and fertilising weeds instead of giving God's seed the run of the garden, with uncluttered space to grow and develop towards fruitfulness (Matthew 13:7, 22)?

There are other possibilities: those who have been abused, whether spiritually, sexually or in other ways, may struggle with yielding to Jesus and receiving his life-giving Spirit. Many dear people who have suffered in these ways despair of ever being fruitful. If this describes you, take heart! Lay hold of the truth that all God's children have been raised up, through Christ, to bear fruit (Romans 7:4). Don't let anyone tell you otherwise! If you know your spirit has been crushed or your heart feels like the contaminated, desert-waste aftermath of a nuclear explosion rather than fruitful ground, may I encourage you to seek help? Look for those who have a track record in coming alongside women and men who know they are broken; seek out gentle people who are experienced in ministering the life and hope that comes from the God of hope.

Whatever the problem has been—whether it's teaching centred on right-doing, leaving us stranded up the creek of 'trying harder', or whether it's the sins of others, leaving life-strangling ties to the dominion of darkness—Jesus Christ has the power to save and deliver and to bring a new heredity. No one who comes to him looking for healing and freedom will be turned away.

Fruit, glorious fruit!

At the close of each chapter, I've tried to express something of the nature of the fruit of the Spirit. There may be value in reviewing those sections now, bearing in mind the fact that Paul referred to fruit, not fruits. It's not a fruit bowl from which we may select elements that appeal to us or are in harmony with our personalities, leaving the rest for others. This fruit is the character of Christ, the family likeness, which the Holy Spirit is working to form in us—in you and me—in its entirety.

Does that sound wonderful, or totally impossible? If the latter, call to mind the fact that we're considering fruit, not a self-funded programme of personal improvement. God supplies the seed, the nourishment and the watering. Our responsibility is to open the soil of our hearts to all three and to cooperate with the Master Gardener in the cultivation. If my emphasis on this feels unnecessarily repetitive, please spare a thought for others whose automatic response tends to be, 'But I'll never manage that. I can't!' followed either by a resolve to try harder or by despair. You undoubtedly know someone who struggles in this way—probably several people. If you ask him, God will attune your ears so that you may pick up on the battles of one or two others, opening the way for you to encourage them in their desire to be fruitful.

Galatians 5:22–23 is the only passage that refers specifically to the fruit 'of the Spirit', but there are others that bring complementary insights. For example, Paul tells Timothy to 'pursue righteousness, godliness, faith, love, endurance and gentleness', and to 'pursue righteousness, faith, love and peace, along with those who call on the Lord out of a pure heart' (1 Timothy 6:11; 2 Timothy 2:22). Paul exhorts the Christians at Ephesus to 'live as children of light', adding that 'the fruit of the light consists in all goodness, righteousness and truth' (Ephesians 5:8–9). He tells them to 'find out what pleases the Lord' (v. 10)—wise advice! In this, the scriptures are an indispensable guide.

Leaving a wake

Let's turn for a moment to a different lens through which to view some additional aspects of bearing fruit for God's kingdom. Throughout his book *Integrity*, Dr Henry Cloud likens the imprint we leave on the world as we pass through it to the wake of a boat. We may be tempted to assume that any sort of wake—any sort of disturbance left behind— must be undesirable for a follower of Jesus, but this is not a biblical view. Visualise Jesus going from town to town with his disciples, touching and socialising with outcasts, debating with religious experts, and then entering Jerusalem. He definitely left a wake!

How may we characterise Jesus' wake? First, there was grace

and truth (John 1:14). The 'truth' part wasn't always welcome; that inevitably produced turbulence. But although Jesus confronted numerous powerful and influential people with (to them) unpalatable truths, to those who were marginalised—those without power or influence—he brought grace upon grace. To many, he brought a mixture: Jesus spoke both grace and truth to the woman at the well and to the woman taken in adultery (John 4:7–18; 8:7–11). (Few would have expected such women to be recipients of grace.) Jesus also showed grace to the powerful when they came to him in the right spirit (for example, the centurion in Luke 7:1–10 and the Pharisee Nicodemus in John 3:1–21). Sometimes the truth Jesus brought was disturbing; sometimes his grace was equally disturbing! The question for us is this: 'Is my wake also characterised by both grace and truth?'

Second, there was the wake left by Jesus' servant-heartedness (Luke 22:25–27; Philippians 2:5–8). This disposition becomes apparent when the self-giving, undefeatable goodwill of *agape* love reveals itself in actions that serve another person or the common good, to the glory of God. 'Having a servant heart' is not to be confused with 'rushing round doing lots of jobs': whether we are busy or at rest, a servant heart is still a servant heart. Jesus allowed men and women to serve him on occasions that are recorded in scripture (for example, Luke 4:39; John 12:2) and, no doubt, on many others, too. A truly servant-hearted person will not insist on always being in the role of helper. (Those who are reluctant to be helped or served by others often find accepting help from God very difficult as well.) You may find it constructive to reread the sections about the various aspects of the fruit of the Spirit with servant-heartedness in mind; they all have relevance to this disposition.

Servant-hearted leadership was a challenge for Jesus' first disciples and remains so today. Having explained that he was facing death, Jesus found his friends arguing about which of them was the greatest. Jesus responded, 'If anyone wants to be first, he must be the very last, and the servant of all' (Mark 9:35), but they just didn't get it. It was so totally different from the mindset they'd absorbed while growing up; their minds were unaccustomed to 'bending' in that direction. Jesus was still dealing with their hopes of status—in the case of James and John, the request that they might sit either side of him in the top seat—as he headed towards Jerusalem for the final time (Mark 10:32–45). You could pause and ask yourself, 'Is servant-heartedness revealed by my wake?'

God-focused fruit-bearing

We've already looked in some detail at how we may be transformed through worship and prayer. I return to them now because they foster God-consciousness rather than self-consciousness. With a right view of God and ourselves, our potential for fruitfulness grows, but there's more to it: with worship and prayer threading through our lives, we're less likely to become a distraction to others, saying (in effect, if not in words), 'Look at me and my fruit!' Worship and prayer act as preservatives for the fruit we are bearing, stopping it from going mouldy and drawing people's eyes away from God and on to us. This is vital if we're to bear 'fruit that will last' (John 15:16; 'fruit that won't spoil', THE MESSAGE).

Fruit borne in a God-focused life brings glory to him. Any praise or thankfulness expressed toward us is swiftly and unself-consciously incorporated in worship and thanksgiving to God, forming part of our continual offering of 'a sacrifice of praise—the fruit of lips that confess his name' (Hebrews 13:15).

God-focused worship and prayer also foster true humility, another characteristic of Jesus. He was prepared to stand his ground when that was called for, and he didn't downplay his identity or his role, so what did Jesus mean when he described himself as humble (Matthew 11:29)? Jesus used two complementary words when he said, 'I am gentle [*praus*; also translated 'humble': see pages 137–138] and humble [*tapeinos*] in heart.' *Tapeinos* (also translated 'lowly') describes a person who does not work towards self-aggrandisement or pursue status (see John the Baptist's attitude, John 3:30), someone who is willing to associate with people whom others see as of little importance (Romans 12:16).

Sadly, for many people, humility is epitomised not by Jesus but by the Dickens character Uriah Heep, a master of insincere grovelling—which has nothing to do with humility. In Paul's day, humility was not universally held to be a virtue. Never the less, he urged the Ephesians, as part of living a life worthy of their calling, to be 'completely humble and gentle' (Ephesians 4:2; see also Philippians 2:3 and the virtues listed in Colossians 3:12). Why not review these scriptures, inviting God to speak further about being more conscious of him than of yourself?

Peter advised, 'Humble yourselves, therefore, under God's mighty hand,' swiftly followed by, 'Cast all your anxiety on him because he cares for you' (1 Peter 5:6–7). Have you ever noticed the juxtaposition? Dallas Willard writes, 'Humility is a great secret of rest of soul because it does not presume to secure outcomes' (*Renovation of the Heart*, p. 210). The truth that God is almighty and in control can settle my inner being—I don't *have* to be anxious—and humility also allows me to know and be content with the fact that I don't have to make it all happen! It's perfectly safe for me to take time for sabbath rest, for play, for eating (sitting down, chewing each mouthful properly) and for sleep, because he is God and I am not. With my eyes on Jesus, I love, I give, I serve, I obey and I rest, leaving the outcomes to him. Humility allows God to be God and enthrones Jesus as king.

Let's turn now to courage. Ancient philosophical traditions listed this as one of the virtues, and Christians have long recognised it as a characteristic that our heavenly Father forms in his children by his Spirit. It often takes courage as well as humility to hear and obey and then leave the outcome to God. By taking Jesus at his word and yielding to him, some of his followers have gone on to live extraordinary lives and to bear fruit on an unimaginable scale.

Jewish leaders and scholars were astonished by the courage of Peter and John. They 'took note' that these 'unschooled, ordinary men... had been with Jesus' (Acts 4:13). After being imprisoned, told to speak no more about Jesus and threatened by powerful people, Peter and John returned to the other believers. Instead of panicking, they joined in God-focused worship and prayer:

'Now, Lord, consider their threats and enable your servants to speak your word with great boldness. Stretch out your hand to heal

and perform miraculous signs and wonders through the name of your holy servant Jesus.' After they prayed, the place where they were meeting was shaken. And they were all filled with the Holy Spirit and spoke the word of God boldly. (vv. 29–31)

It still takes courage, in many parts of the world, for brothers and sisters in Christ to speak the name of Jesus, even among family and friends. I am challenged by what I read in Acts 4 and by stories of the many believers who have lived humbly and died courageously since. Am I—are you—ready to pray the prayer those early Christians prayed?

Praying for fruitfulness

In my experience, prayers for one another tend to be more problem-orientated than fruit-orientated. It would be good to develop a habit of praying for fruitfulness, especially as much of what Paul has to say about fruit comes in the context of praying for it to increase. Along with Timothy, he writes to the Colossians:

We have not stopped praying for you and asking God to fill you with the knowledge of his will through all spiritual wisdom and understanding… in order that you may live a life worthy of the Lord and may please him in every way: bearing fruit in every good work, growing in the knowledge of God, being strengthened with all power according to his glorious might so that you may have great endurance and patience, and joyfully giving thanks to the Father, who has qualified you to share in the inheritance of the saints in the kingdom of light. (1:9–12)

That's some prayer! Have you ever realised that members of your home group or family could pray like this for one another?

In a letter addressed to 'all the saints in Christ Jesus at Philippi', Paul writes, 'And this is my prayer: that your love may abound more and more in knowledge and depth of insight, so that you may be able to discern what is best and may be pure and blameless until the day of Christ, filled with the fruit of righteousness that comes through Jesus Christ—to the glory and praise of God' (Philippians 1:1, 9–11). That's another great prayer to pray for one another.

We need to learn not just to pray, 'Lord, please take away the pain' for each other when we could also be praying, 'Lord, please make this difficult time fruitful.' Troubles, remember, may be used to develop 'passionate patience' and to forge 'the tempered steel of virtue' (Romans 5:3–4, THE MESSAGE). Have you ever prayed in this way? Can you think of times when such prayer has been fruitful?

In 1949, my husband Stephen was on board a plane that crashed in the Pennines. Many were killed, including his younger brother, Roger. Stephen and his parents spent weeks in hospital. Shortly after his sixth birthday, they were visited by a missionary friend who said, 'It's time to start praying for Stephen's future wife.' Not the usual hospital chit-chat, I think you'll agree! But this wasn't just about making conversation: within a matter of days, I was to be born. After Stephen and I were married, I discovered that I'd been prayed for by his parents for my whole life.

Overwhelmed by their injuries and the loss of their two-year-old son, Jim and Ruth could have allowed God's prompting to be sidelined. Tragedy could have become the emblem of their lives. Among all the 'Why?' questions, they could have distanced themselves from God, but they didn't. My in-laws never told me what they prayed for me, but, whatever it was, I'm grateful. I have no doubt that their prayers were fruitful—in my life and also in theirs as they walked forward in trusting obedience.

How about praying the following prayer for those you know who are facing difficulties? You could pray it for yourself, for those you love and perhaps also for those who may one day become members of your family through marriage: 'Gracious Father, please expand their / my capacity to receive from you, according to your great riches, that they / I may be fruitful, bearing fruit that lasts and brings you glory.'

Abiding, obeying, loving and bearing fruit

Half a lifetime ago, I was a mum with two small children. After I'd been reading John 15 one day, God gave me a picture of something that I can only describe as part-vine and part-apple tree. The gnarled trunk was composed of three intertwined parts, labelled 'abiding', 'obeying' and 'loving'. Spread across the canopy were the words 'bearing fruit'. Reading the same passage today in a modern version, I can still see this picture.

'I am the Real Vine and my Father is the Farmer... Live in me. Make your home in me just as I do in you... you can't bear fruit unless you are joined with me. I am the Vine, you are the branches. When you're joined with me and I with you, the relation intimate and organic, the harvest is sure to be abundant... if you make

yourselves at home with me and my words are at home in you, you can be sure that whatever you ask will be listened to and acted upon. This is how my Father shows who he is—when you produce grapes, when you mature as my disciples. I've loved you the way my Father has loved me. Make yourselves at home in my love. If you keep my commands, you'll remain intimately at home in my love. That's what I've done—kept my Father's commands and made myself at home in his love.'

JOHN 15:1, 4–5, 7–10 (*THE MESSAGE*)

Jesus says to each one of us, 'When you're joined with me and I with you, the relation intimate and organic, the harvest is sure to be abundant' (v. 5). If you remember nothing else from this chapter, I hope you'll remember these encouraging words.

BIBLE REFLECTIONS

1. Read Psalm 92.

Reread verses 12–15, if possible in a variety of translations. In the natural world, fruit trees may be uprooted after a while to make room for new ones. Yet in God's kingdom the mature among us have no need to see our fruitful years as past, and no one is too young to bear fruit. Use these verses as a springboard into a dialogue with God about fruitfulness in his kingdom. As you go through the next few days, ask him to draw to your attention any blind spots or prejudices that have been distorting your perception or your understanding of who may or can bear fruit, and how it may or must be done. In this psalm, righteousness is the stated characteristic of the fruit-bearers. How does this sit with your attitude to fruitfulness?

2. Word search: *akarpos* (unfruitful).

Read the verses listed below, along with the verses surrounding them to give the context. Make notes on the conditions causing or contributing to a lack of fruit. (Leave room for further notes to be added later.)

- Matthew 13:22 and Mark 4:19 (from the parable of the sower)
- Ephesians 5:11 ('fruitless deeds of darkness')
- Titus 3:14 and 2 Peter 1:8 (where *akarpos* is translated 'unproductive')

Thinking back to what you read in the previous chapter about spiritual disciplines, how might God want to use one or more of these disciplines to promote fruitfulness in you? Use the notes you have made as a starting point for a conversation with your heavenly Father, and note down what he says to you.

3. Read John 15:1–17.

On a large piece of paper, write out verses 1–8 or 9–17, leaving as much space as possible around the sides and between the lines. (You could do the same with the other verses on another occasion.) Ask God to speak to you through particular words and phrases, and see which he highlights. In the adjacent free space, make notes or sketch images as they come to mind. This is a 'reflection' rather than a study, so keep your heart engaged. I recommend coming back to it over a period of time, rather than trying to cover every aspect in one session.

Remembering that we may expect the characteristics of Christ to be formed in us as we yield to the Spirit of Jesus, and that 'we're considering fruit, not a self-funded programme of personal improvement', take time to decide how you would like to pray. Even if you don't normally write down your prayers, it may be worth doing so on this occasion—so that you may pray it regularly over time and spot the answers as they come. You could ask a friend to pray for you and to keep in touch, so that he or she may encourage you over the next few months as you seek God and welcome the fruitfulness he brings.

✳

EPILOGUE

Since this is the kind of life we have chosen, the life of the Spirit, let us make sure that we do not just hold it as an idea in our heads or a sentiment in our hearts, but work out its implications in every detail of our lives.

GALATIANS 5:25 (*THE MESSAGE*)

Anyone who claims to be intimate with God ought to live the same kind of life Jesus lived.

1 JOHN 2:6 (*THE MESSAGE*)

The challenge is clear, but where to start? Paul advised, 'Watch what God does, and then you do it, like children who learn proper behaviour from their parents. Mostly what God does is love you. Keep company with him and learn a life of love' (Ephesians 5:1–2, *THE MESSAGE*). As we keep company with God, we may have confidence that he will reveal the way forward.

You've probably been aware of God highlighting at least one issue already, so that's the place to begin—maybe re-reading the relevant part of the book or mulling over what you wrote in your journal. If, for example, you recognised a tendency to make do with the spiritual equivalent of a dry biscuit, how about developing the habit of asking Father God if he has more for you? If what you read about self-justification or self-pity rang bells, you could ask him at the end of each day to bring to mind any occasions when these blockages to God's grace have intruded. Whether or not these specific examples are relevant to you, taking a moment before sleep to seek God's forgiveness, and to give thanks for evidences of his grace and mercy, is always a blessing.

Each of us needs to develop the habit of listening to 'the One who created us, formed us, and loves us as we are and yet always seeks to lead us to become more than we are' (Job, *Three Simple Rules*, p. 8). Why not tell God that you're ready to hear more, that you want to go on hearing words from his heart about your heart and to cooperate with his plans to make your life more fruitful for his kingdom?

If you'd like to take up the suggestion of praying for one another to be fruitful, you could use the sections on the fruit of the Spirit week by week in your group as a prelude to prayer. You might also like to consider whether you're willing to work at encouraging each other to stay faithful, both in the good times and when enduring 'the sandpaper of failure and frustration'. Paul, Peter and the other disciples weren't afraid of speaking and writing in ways designed to spur on their brothers and sisters in Christ, urging them to 'live lives worthy of God' (1 Thessalonians 2:12). These days, we're comfortable with sympathy and empathy but far less comfortable with urging one another on.

Paul was able to see the purposes of God being worked out on a scale that most of us find hard to imagine. He told the Ephesians of God's intention that 'now, through the church, the manifold wisdom of God should be made known to the rulers and authorities in the heavenly realms, according to his eternal purpose which he accomplished in Christ Jesus our Lord' (Ephesians 3:10–11). This passage culminates in a triumphant acclamation: 'Now to him who is able to do immeasurably more than all we ask or imagine, according to his power that is at work within us, to him be glory in the church and in Christ Jesus throughout all generations, for ever and ever! Amen' (vv. 20–21). Amen, indeed!

Spirit of Jesus, you are welcome in my heart and in my home. I yield to you. May your life in me shape the way I am, and the way I live.

✳

BIBLIOGRAPHY

David Augsburger, *Dissident Discipleship: A spirituality of self-surrender, love of God, and love of neighbour* (Brazos Press, 2006)

William Barclay, *Flesh and Spirit: An examination of Galatians 5:19–23* (SCM Press, 1962)

Dietrich Bonhoeffer, *The Cost of Discipleship* (SCM Press, 2001)

Dietrich Bonhoeffer, *Life Together* (SCM Press,1954)

Paul Bradbury, *Life from Death Emerging* (Triangle, 2002)

Brother Lawrence, *The Practice of the Presence of God*, trans. E.M. Blaiklock (Hodder and Stoughton, 1981)

Oswald Chambers, *My Utmost for His Highest* (special updated edition), ed. James Reimann (Discovery House, 1995)

Guy Chevreau, *Vital Signs of a Healthy Church* (New Wine Ministries, 2007)

Henry Cloud, *Integrity: The courage to meet the demands of reality* (Collins, 2006)

Pamela Evans, *Driven Beyond the Call of God: Discovering the rhythms of grace* (BRF, 1999)

Pamela Evans, *Building the Body: Transforming relationships in the local church* (BRF, 2002)

Richard Foster, *Celebration of Discipline: The path to spiritual growth* (Hodder and Stoughton, 1980)

Thomas H. Green, *Darkness in the Marketplace: The Christian at prayer in the world* (Ave Maria Press, 1981)

James Davison Hunter, *The Death of Character: Moral education in an age without good or evil* (Basic Books, 2000)

Rueben P. Job, *Three Simple Rules: A Wesleyan way of living* (Abingdon Press, 2007)

C.S. Lewis, *Letters to Malcolm: Chiefly on Prayer* (Geoffrey Bles, 1964)

Thomas Merton, *New Seeds of Contemplation* (New Directions, 1972)

J. Philip Newell, *Celtic Prayers from Iona* (Paulist Press, 1997)

Ian Stackhouse, *The Day is Yours: Slow spirituality in a fast-moving world* (Paternoster, 2008)

David H. Stern, *Jewish New Testament Commentary* (Jewish New Testament Publications, 1992)

A.W. Tozer, *The Worship-Driven Life*, ed. James L. Snyder (Monarch, 2008)

Keith J. White, *The Growth of Love: Understanding five essential elements of child development* (BRF, 2008)

Dallas Willard, *Renovation of the Heart: Putting on the character of Christ* (NavPress, 2002)

Dallas Willard, *The Spirit of the Disciplines: Understanding how God changes lives* (Hodder and Stoughton, 1996)

Other books

Steve Dixon, *Lifepath: A Land of Broken Vows* (Scripture Union, 2009). Part of the Lifepath Adventures series, this novel for children, set in twelfth-century England, incorporates themes relating to promises being kept and broken.

James Lawrence, *Growing Leaders: Reflections on leadership, life and Jesus* (BRF, 2004). This book and the CPAS course *Growing Leaders* focus on the character development of leaders.

C.S. Lewis, *Mere Christianity* (numerous editions available). Rereading this after many years, I found it a refreshing antidote to flabby and crooked thinking about our faith and what it means to be a disciple of Jesus.

DISCOVERING THE SPIRITUAL EXERCISES OF SAINT IGNATIUS

LARRY WARNER

This book is an adaptation of the Spiritual Exercises of St Ignatius Loyola, to help you to embark on a life-transforming journey toward Christlikeness. For nearly 500 years, the Exercises have been a tool for spiritual formation. During those years their popularity has ebbed and flowed, but they are now experiencing something of a revival across the breadth of the Church.

This is not a book about the methods or techniques of Christian formation but one that enables you to come before God through the Gospel narratives in order to encounter Jesus afresh. If you hunger for something deeper, yearn to walk with Jesus (not just read about him) and desire to embrace more of what God is doing in and through you, then this is the book for you.

ISBN 978 1 84101 883 6   £10.99
Available from www.brfonline.org.uk, or from your local Christian bookshop.

PRAYER

Steps to a deeper relationship

HENRY FRENCH

This book is about how to embark on the path of prayer, the way that will lead you closer and closer to the heart of God if you follow it faithfully and patiently. Grounded in scripture, each chapter is filled with wise advice, plus exercises to build confidence not only in intercession, but also meditative prayer and journal-keeping. The aim is always to show how making space for prayer is not only an essential spiritual discipline but a source of deep joy. The book concludes with a further section of helpful ideas and suggestions to put into practice what you have learned.

ISBN 978 1 84101 861 4   £6.99

Available from www.brfonline.org.uk, or from your local Christian bookshop.

WORKING FROM A PLACE OF REST

Jesus and the key to sustaining ministry

TONY HORSFALL

Exhaustion, burnout, tiredness, even breakdown... sadly such conditions are all too common these days, not least among those involved in some kind of Christian ministry, whether full-time, part-time or voluntary. In striving to do our utmost for God, we can easily forget that there were many times when Jesus himself was willing to rest, to do nothing except wait for the Spirit's prompting, so that he demonstrated the vital principle of 'working from a place of rest'.

Drawing on extensive experience of training and mentoring across the world, Tony Horsfall reflects on the story of Jesus and the Samaritan woman to draw out practical guidance for sustainable Christian life and work.

ISBN 978 1 84101 544 6   £6.99
Available from www.brfonline.org.uk, or from your local Christian bookshop.

A HEART TO LISTEN

Becoming a listening person in a noisy world

MICHAEL MITTON

Listening has become a lost art in a world that is growing ever noisier, more superficial and more stressed. Too many of us have forgotten not only about listening to others but also about listening to God, our own hearts, our wider communities, and even our planet. Without listening, how can we hope to gain wisdom, to build deep and truly caring relationships with all kinds of people, to share our faith?

This accessible book shows how, with God's help, we can relearn the art of listening and in doing so become a source of help and healing for others and for ourselves. Biblical reflection is interwoven with insights from the author's wide experience of listening ministry in the UK and abroad. Between the chapters are episodes of an intriguing story, which explores the book's themes through vividly imagined characters in a cross-cultural setting.

ISBN 978 1 84101 269 8   £7.99

Available from www.brfonline.org.uk, or from your local Christian bookshop.

GROWING LEADERS

Reflections on leadership, life and Jesus

JAMES LAWRENCE

Seven out of ten Christian leaders feel overworked, four in ten suffer financial pressures, only two in ten have had management training, and 1500 give up their job over a ten-year period. At the same time, as financial restrictions affect the availability of full-time ministers, more people are needed for leadership roles in local congregations, for every area of church work.

This book faces the challenge of raising up new leaders and helping existing leaders to mature, using the model for growing leaders at the heart of the Arrow Leadership Programme, a ministry of the Church Pastoral Aid Society (CPAS). It comprehensively surveys leadership skills and styles, discerning our personal calling, avoiding the 'red zone' of stress, developing character, and living as part of the community of God's people.

ISBN 978 1 84101 246 9   £8.99
Available from www.brfonline.org.uk, or from your local Christian bookshop.

THE GROWTH OF LOVE

Understanding five essential elements of child development

KEITH J. WHITE

This book is designed to be essential reading for those involved in the pastoral care of chldren. However, all of us have a part to play in creating the global village in which love and, by implication, children can best thrive.

The Growth of Love, based on a lifetime's experience of caring for children whose own families have become stressed or broken, draws on the literature of child development and psychiatry, the daily practice of residential and foster care, and the resources and experience of the Judeo-Christian faith. It describes five elements that all three confirm are vital to human development and provides practical insights into what constitutes 'good enough' parenting and care. Where these elements—security, boundaries, significance, community and creativity—are present, love is able to grow.

ISBN 978 1 84101 461 6   £8.99
Available from www.brfonline.org.uk, or from your local Christian bookshop.

About

BRF is a registered charity and also a limited company, and has been in existence since 1922. Through all that we do—producing resources, providing training, working face-to-face with adults and children, and via the web— we work to resource individuals and church communities in their Christian discipleship through the Bible, prayer and worship.

Our Barnabas children's team works with primary schools and churches to help children under 11, and the adults who work with them, to explore Christianity creatively and to bring the Bible alive.

To find out more about BRF and its core activities and ministries, visit:

www.brf.org.uk
www.brfonline.org.uk
www.biblereadingnotes.org.uk
www.barnabasinschools.org.uk
www.barnabasinchurches.org.uk
www.faithinhomes.org.uk
www.messychurch.org.uk
www.foundations21.org.uk

If you have any questions about BRF and our work, please email us at

enquiries@brf.org.uk